A Client A Day...
The Coffee Shop Way

by
Tonya Hofmann

Published by
High Hopes Publishing
1618 Williams Drive #5
Georgetown, TX 78628
(512) 868-0548
www.highhopespublishing.com

This book is intended as an overview of the topic by the author. No claim is made that the information is suitable for every person under every situation. It is the responsibility of the reader to ascertain if the information contained within is appropriate. Liability will not be assumed for any loss or damage incurred by the use of the material herein.

ISBN 978-0-9708417-9-7

This book is available at quantity discounts for bulk purchases.

For information, contact High Hopes Publishing at

1-888-742-0074.

Acknowledgements

I want to thank my sister, Dr. Rhonda Blackburn for her support and for telling me in person "I'm proud of you!" What an impact and inspiration you have made in my life!

I want to thank my husband, Michael Hofmann who has always let me be who I am and also helped me see who I can be.

I want to thank my good friend, Gene Vasconi and editor of my book for encouraging me and helping me through this much-longer-than-was-ever-expected process! I know the chipmunks are clapping (private joke)!

INTRODUCTION

I hear people quote book after book after book that they have read on personal development and marketing their business; however, they rarely implement anything they learn in the books into their lives and their business. I have found that most people become overwhelmed with information and can't figure out how to digest it into their lives. I want to give you simple but effective information to help you immediately make a difference and give you incredible results. BUT, I want to give you a warning... I don't sugar coat and this is real information in all its raw complication and beauty.

So, you may be asking, who in the heck is this lady? Who is Tonya Hofmann?

I'm a natural introvert even though when you meet me you would swear that I've never had a hard time interacting with people, presenting at the front of the room or talking to strangers. I had a very difficult childhood, been robbed and tied up, had cancer and those aren't even the worst things so when I say "If I can do it, you can do it!" I really mean it. If you said in 2005 I would be where I am now, I would have thought you were crazy. All the information I've learned and taken action on in my life and my businesses can be achieved by anyone. You just need to know the right formula and be able to take action yourself.

I started out in the clothing industry working at a boutique in the mall while I was in high school and continued there for five years. I quickly became one of the top sales associates in the country. I learned how to sell and what to focus on when it came to helping clients and reaching the goal for that day which was always a total of how much you personally rang up. It was a great training ground and crash course into the world of making people happy which is the true essence of a sale. I then became a manager of a small mom and pop store in the mall that sold science and nature products. At 25 years old, I bought the business from them with my husband, Michael. We were two kids that were so excited about all the possibilities of being entrepreneurs. It had been a lifelong dream of mine. Then the reality of business hit us square in the face. The old owners ran off to Hawaii and weren't there to give us advice, training or just be someone to ask questions of. We didn't know that we could have negotiated the price of the sale, the training on how to run the store, order products, negotiate lease space or anything that would have helped us be successful. We made a lot of mistakes but also learned a lot of valuable information and figured out what did work. We took the store to a half a million dollars in sales and opened up a second location. After 7 years and deciding that Houston wasn't where we wanted to raise our daughter, we decided to close up shop and move to Austin, TX.

We were so excited to start something new but didn't know what the next step was or the next business we wanted to start. We went into the work force. I was a contract sales rep for a wholesale gift industry showroom. I traveled around Texas helping small to large retail stores that carried any type of gift items such as teddy bears, wind chimes, knick knacks, Christmas items and so on. I found that I loved traveling and helping people to make decision about orchestrating a great selling season. I helped them navigate through what they "liked" and wanted to bring into their store versus what I saw selling fast in the market place. My work assisted the manufacturers that I represented to get their products out to market and I gave them feedback as to what I heard as a "want" in the market place.

My husband, Michael went into computers, management, HR and soon into helping a small start up Website Company go from $800,000 a year to over 16 million. He helped construct websites and software programs for large business and the government. He saw the changes in the industry, the differences between programmers, the ability to create a program that could do amazing things and simplify huge projects at a push of a button. He became incredibly fascinated with programming and started learning it on his own. Michael was ecstatic and proud when he created his first HTML page. We look back and think that it was nothing but without that first step, he wouldn't be where he is today. Now he has the ability to create anything needed in the web world. It has been exciting to watch his learning growth.

YES, I LOVE having a GEEK in my corner! He comes in quite handy.

We had always wanted to work together again and looked at all kinds of possibilities of our next venture together. On the way back from San Angelo, TX (not a whole lot to do driving by yourself in West Texas) I had an idea. We were very successful in marketing in our retail stores and Michael was fantastic at websites so we figured, "why not start a company helping all the small business owners I knew develop a powerful website and market their company on a directory website of our own?" So, Michael created a website called www.YourLocalCity.com where we sold advertising and memberships so that business owners could get some great online marketing for their products and services. Michael continued to produce incredible websites for small to large companies but I started networking to get the message out about my new venture. I really fell in love with networking and joined 54 different networking groups, associations and chambers across the Austin, TX area. Yes, that is right... 54!!! I couldn't believe it either until I started counting them all up one day. One thing I realized about networking: there were a lot of groups I didn't fit into, didn't like, or wasn't getting any results from. Because I always look for ways to enhance or improve things I see, I decided to start my own networking group. I would take out everything I didn't like about networking and keep and enhance everything I loved. I grew my networking organization into and around the four largest cities in Texas. Then, in Spring of 2011, I met one of my new competitors that had just rolled into town from Las Vegas. She had a national networking group organization and I offered to sell her my groups to give her a quick jump into the Texas market. She agreed and I sold the networking groups of *Your Local City* to Biz Pack and Defining Women's network in March of 2011.

One reason I sold was so I could have more time to help people develop their business and their websites and the networking groups were very time-consuming. It was a perfect marriage of the groups and perfect timing. I had been developing a new concept called *Stand Out In Your Business* that would give business owners access to incredible experts and information that would help them grow their business. It even had a component

6

where they could market their business and help it grow while sharing revenues when they referred businesses who wanted websites, coaching or a *Stand Out* product from one of our experts. *Stand Out In Your Business* was an immediate success by giving people the vehicle to do to create multiple income streams while transforming their beliefs and habits. Your Local City continues to this day as an advertising vehicle for businesses and creation of websites that truly drive traffic.

I've been speaking across Texas at local networking groups and conferences but wanted to take it up a notch and in 4 short months I started to get booked across the nation and even internationally. Helping people figure out my secrets and formulas to increase visibility, increase new clients, increase success is one of the areas I offered and want to offer you in this book. I love giving people the information that will transform their lives in all aspects of their business because it has helped me transform mine.

I hate being bored so I started a new business networking group called the *Organization Of Power Partners*. It was a combination of everything that I have learned about what people wanted in and out of networking groups. I also included areas to help give the members great insight into many areas for their business success. We combined everything we were successful at in *Your Local City* and *Stand Out In Your Business* so that they got three main areas of growth: Connections to Experts, Networking with Referrals, and Marketing. Because I've been flying around the country meeting so many truly gifted and knowledgeable experts in all kinds of business fields and industry, it was only natural that I brought them in as Mentors. I understood that most people couldn't afford to hire my national friends which usually charged $10,000 or more for coaching but what I had worked out with them was to coach my members through webinars and teleconferences to give insight and the latest information out there on all kinds of business arenas. With the networking component, I wanted it to be different than what anyone was used to attending. I knew that people in a group usually became friends and were very social but I wanted the groups to be focused on business. If I took time out of my business day to network and I asked others to do the same, there had better be a great business benefit attached to it.

There was no elevator pitch fest at the groups, rather full minutes of information from every member to give the group insight into what each person offered and sold. The whole meeting was about the members and their business with a fun twist with topics to go over at each meeting.

And then there was marketing. One area I knew that was hard for business owners was finding new clients. At first, you go through your family and friends and then what? Well, we created a huge, easy to use, online business directory so that everyone could easily find one another in the networking realm. Each person's directory ad was able to be pulled up in the internet searches they did. We wanted anyone and everyone to be able to find amazing people that had incredible products or services to offer the public or other businesses.

OPP was up and running and continues to provide an exceptional service to all its members to this day. This only highlights a small part of what we offer. If you are interested, go to www.OrganizationOfPowerPartners.com.

My favorite quote is,
"Life isn't about finding yourself, life is about creating yourself!"
So who do you want to create?

 **Chapter 1**

"No appointment happens without a conversation"

Let's start with the coffee shop.

Why coffee shops? If you are some place where you meet people who are your target market, then you have the ability to meet a new client that day and a coffee shop is the perfect place. Who goes to one? If you really look at most people who hang out at coffee shops, they are students, small business owners, sales reps and people meeting each other for a purpose. So for me this is exactly my target market: I hang out there, have all my meetings there, do business there and enjoy having some fantastic conversations. I have more than one really amazing daily miracle! A sale, a new business alliance and an offer or connection to someone or something I need to know. It has been a gold mine. But, if you start hanging out in a place and you are there to just sell then don't bother. People can see circling vultures from a mile away. I'm going to show you exactly how to do all the above without ever appearing to circle!

At a coffee shop one day, I overheard a lady behind me talk about her business. I was actually interested in talking to her about what she did and finding out more about her product. When the person she was talking to left, I turned around to ask her for information and immediately just smiled and turned right back around. Why you might ask? She was sitting there with a jogging outfit on and when I smiled at her she didn't smile back but kept a frown with a "what are you looking at" question on her face. She completely missed an opportunity to have me as a new client.

So let's talk about what is first...what you look like. Yep, that comes first. Don't expect to do business in sweat pants. You have to look the part. Also, make sure you are always wearing your most important accessory: your smile! No one wants to talk to someone who isn't happy and doesn't look successful.

Are you a believer that if it happens it is suppose to be? Well, if you don't look the part and aren't talking to anyone there is no way that will occur! You have to initiate something for anything to happen. Doing something positive receives something positive and negative receives negative. Think about it. If you saw someone come up to you and they looked grumpy or bored, would you want to talk to them? If they looked like they just rolled out of bed, would you want to talk to them about their business? Doubtful. Just because you own your own business and do business at a coffee shop doesn't mean you should look like a student who just rolled out of bed or isn't ready to do business. Since you do own your own business now, it doesn't mean you get to slack off. What it means is that you have to prove yourself even more every single day. You have to work harder than you have ever worked before. Why wouldn't you? If you are willing to work eight super hard hours, get dressed up and push to grow a business for someone else, why wouldn't you want to do that and more for yourself?!

So, you need to go in expecting that you will make something happen today. I go in wanting to walk out with 3 new incredible contacts. I go in prepared. I never go to the mall, the grocery store, the park, the coffee shop, an event... anywhere without being prepared! You should always have your business cards with you. If you have a catalog, a sample or something to hand someone, have it with you! Also, have your appointment calendar with you. The person may not have time to chat right then but if you don't get it on the calendar it will be ten times harder to get it later.

Next, the conversation cannot be about you or your product/service! Look at it this way... if you saw yourself coming, would you say "Hi", would you listen to what you are saying and would you buy from you? Be truly honest with yourself. When you approach someone and if they have a hint that you are trying to sell them, they immediately put up a wall.

You do it too. If someone starts off talking about their self and their product or service you probably say in your head... "Oh, no... they are trying to get me to spend my money!"

It is important to have your hand in the shaking position rather than your palm towards the ceiling!

How can you help someone today? You could be a great resource, have some way to help them or give them some advice or maybe they need something from someone you know. You just have a great conversation and see if you can connect with the new person. Those you don't connect to, just let them go!

So how do you start a conversation? With women it is a little easier since you can comment on their shoes or jewelry even though I've had guys try this and it creeps me out. If the question isn't authentic to you, it will come across as forced or just weird. Talk about the weather, about the place you are in or whatever you can pull from. Have questions ready in your head. My favorite is, "Do you work around here?" Most people don't mind answering that and it isn't too personal. Most people's identity is wrapped up in what they do for a living so it can really open up to a huge conversation. They usually give you more information that you could have ever asked for. I know from that point what I should continue the conversation or end it. I however never, ever talk about what I do unless they ask me! I have a tendency in my head to go, "Come on... ask me what I do... come on.... COME ON...!" But I can't come across as being there for any reason but than to meet someone else or do some work. Not until they get curious as to what I do that I can tell them. Because again, if someone starts spewing all about their product and service to you and you didn't want to know, then you aren't going to be thrilled with that person and you certainly won't buy from them. If though, you were curious and did ask them what they did then you have a different mind set. At that moment, it is about what you want and not what they want.

It is hard though. Doesn't it drive you crazy that everyone isn't excited as you are about your company? But then again, you aren't excited about everyone else's company. You are simply trying to weed through the possibilities to find your perfect client. Don't let your sales person side come out until it is appropriate. The rule of letting them talk and you not saying anything until they ask works on so many levels. I use it all the time. At networking events, conferences, coffee shops, parking lots, any place where people didn't come specifically to hear me talk about my company.

So, first you need the person to look at you. Once you get their attention, then you can ask them your question.

Here is a list of good questions:

1. Do you work around here?
2. Did I meet you at that _____?
   (networking event, conference, church, kids school, etc.)
3. Have you heard of this upcoming _____?
   (event, networking meeting, conference, presentation, kids activities, church function, etc.)
4. Where did you get that _____?
   (skirt, shoes, jewelry)
   This then goes into I just bought a new (whatever) for my next presentation or event or whatever you are up to.

With the last question you can see how the conversation must continue on. How are you going to tie it into your business, product, service or activity? If you know what your question is then you know what you are going to say next. Again, it must be about them. It can have a slight hint of something you do but that is about it. Until they actually say... "Oh, what do you do?" Then you can actually go into it. But here is the next kicker... it must be really short. If you go into a monologue then their eyes will glaze over and they won't be interested. Keep it short and if they still seem intrigued then see if both of you have some time right then to talk about it or set up an appointment. Don't get so excited that you spill the beans and ruin the sale. Control your excitement and work on the relationship first. They have to know you and like you to buy from you. It is critical that you work through the stages instead of jumping right for the close.

Now you are probably saying, "But I have closed someone right then and there." Yes, so have I but that is a fantastic abnormality that happens every so often that is fun and so exciting when it does happen. This however is not the norm. So always think in your own mind how most people would want you to treat them and to talk to them. Especially when they are about to go into a meeting themselves, are on a nice coffee break, or waiting on a great friend to show up.

As I sit here, I just finished up a one-to-one meeting to get to know a local advertising agent. We were both talking loudly and the lady next to us stood up and asked us for our business cards. She didn't have one in return but you never know what can happen in the future so of course I handed her my card. Who can you connect with today? Well, you will never know until you take action and talk to someone today!

Notes:

Chapter 2

"Simply success; build alliances!"

Relationship Marketing

We usually revert to the old tricks when marketing our product/service. People don't want to be tricked so forget the old way of selling. They want to build a relationship with the sales person (you). The relationship can be a few minutes worth or a few months worth depending on the sales cycle of your industry.

Do you know what the normal sales cycle is for your industry? Ask those who have been doing it a long time and they will know the average length of time it takes to close a sale. That way you are being very realistic with yourself.

Are you taking much longer to complete a sale than usual and if so why?

What is the reality of your industry? This means, if you are marketing your brand new business and it takes two to three years to start making a profit or receive the first sale, are you willing to wait?

People want to buy from someone rather than be sold to. Most people will buy from the person they like the best. Have you ever bought an item from a sales person because they made you feel good? Or you went to several locations and ended up not looking any further because the person helping you was so wonderful? I think everyone has had this experience.

- Do people believe in you?
- Would you buy from yourself?
- Are you creating a person that people want to do business with?

14

- Are you showing benefits rather than features?
- Are you just talking about what *you* want to hear or is it what the client wants to hear?
- Are you waiting on someone to push you?

I believe that coaches are incredibly valuable for accountability purposes. They give you a clear message and an area on which to focus. Most of us can't focus. We often think … I need to do this, this, this, this, this…. and we want to do it all at the same time. The truth is that we can not multitask. You may think you can but are you really accomplishing what you need to do?

Are you finding purpose in everything you do?

Are you focused on what you need to finish, start, develop?

You have to really look at your completion rate. No one else will believe in your business, products and services more than you so would you even hire yourself? This is a harsh reality for most business owners. If you aren't working as hard for yourself as you did for a boss then why are you in business? Did you think you wouldn't have to work that hard?

I met a wonderful man once who told me his story. He went into business with his son. They were doing well but one day his son brought him into the office and told him that he was fired. Now the son really couldn't fire the dad since he was part owner but it was symbolic. He wasn't working hard enough to be an asset to the company and he was causing a lot of problems.

If you don't believe or show passion for your business, who else will? Don't you love being around someone that not only knows their product or service inside and out but when they talk to you they convey the thrill they feel for their company? I know I do.

So be honest with yourself. A lot of people are surprised that they are outsourced, laid off or just passed up for someone else in your industry.

Are you in an entry level position?

Can someone else come in and do what you are producing, selling, offering, filing, cleaning, etc. immediately?

It is the same with your company products or services. Are you offering a service, knowledge or capability that others don't have? Why should they do business with you or keep you in your position at work or hire you for your service or product?

Every time you meet someone you need to showcase these reasons. Give them value. People buy the person instead of just the product so what are you bringing to the table?

When you are buying a dining table, are you buying it for the price, the manufacturer, the sales person, the materials, etc.? It is usually a little of each. Do you not ask if you can you afford it, where and who constructed it, what is the sales person conveying, what is it made of? So look at yourself and ask the same questions about yourself and your product/service: What is the price and who is your target market, are you the manufacture/service provider or where is it constructed/supported, how are you selling them on your product/service and are you answering the questions that they are really asking for, is the quality of your product/service impressive and stand out from your competition?

I was asked to a meeting with a gentleman I knew and he wanted to introduce me to his new company. He showed up with an associate which wasn't a problem but what was the problem was their sales delivery. At first they never asked me about me. Now you need to learn the different types of people. There are those who just want the facts, there are those who want to know about your dog, baby, life and those who want to know what the shiny object is.

I kept asking for the shiny object or the thing that was going to make me go wow. I already knew about the business they were showcasing. Since I already knew about the company, they should have been interested in why I didn't buy originally.

They didn't want to sell to me. Getting together with me is a sales opportunity. They wanted me to attend a meeting on a different day. (I was confused... wasn't I already in a meeting?) Now I'm a busy person and I had already set a lot of time aside to meet with them that day. I wanted them to sell me on their concept. Remember that people want to buy from a person and they didn't want to be that person. They wanted a better "Sales Person" to do the heavy lifting. I just wanted honest information and why they got into it.

They never listened to what I was asking for. I had a particular question and they would not answer my question. They kept dancing around it rather than hitting it head on. Needless to say, I did not buy their service. Don't be afraid to be honest with people. The more upfront and honest you are the better.

Notes:

Chapter 3

"Who did you create as your business persona? You need to LOVE it?"

So why haven't you done more in your life than you have already? Every minute I sat and stared at the TV screen I felt as if I could have been doing something more productive with my time. Now there is a value in down time but too much down time is just excuse time. Most people watch 32 hours of TV a week! Just think of what you could accomplish over your competition if you watched only 20 hours and used the other 12 hours on your business. You'd be able to create programs, do follow ups, develop a webinar or telesummit or any number of amazing benefits for your business.

What is your excuse? The normal ones are money, kids, grandkids, spouse, time, hobbies, work, knowledge, and fear. Mine included just about all of these. I always had an excuse for questions like...

- Why not start a new business?
- Why not do a presentation in front of a group of people?
- Why not learn something new or hire a coach to develop my skills or business?
- Why not have my kids involved?
- Why not be someone who matters and makes people smile?

I finally got tired of the "why nots." I wanted to do something that pushed me out of all of my comfort zones...to do something for me first, for my family second and for the whole of the world third! Why NOT! Yes, you can too. You are no different than me. I have fears that most people wouldn't be able to overcome. I have points of stress that make me fall flat on my back. I have knowledge that only goes so far. I have imperfections and weaknesses that have to be admitted but that can not hold me back.

- What are you going to do?
- What is going to stop you?
- What is going to create an obstacle that is so large that you can't overcome it?

The answer should be ... nothing.
Stop the excuses. Be the entire person you were born to be!

Most of our excuses are really a scheduling issue. We are told as soon as we are born when to do things. In school, work, at most activities they tell you when you need to be some place, when to eat, when to go to the bathroom, when to get off, what time to watch TV for a show, and everything is scheduled. So you may be thinking, I don't have a scheduling issue because my entire life is scheduled. Yes, but things go wrong when you enter into anything different. Did you start your own business or become an outside sales rep where you don't have someone telling you what to do? This is the time when most people find out that they have to have a structured schedule that someone else sets. That is why most people are an employee rather than an entrepreneur. Do you wake up whenever, do you stay in your pajamas, do you take a long lunch while watching a TV program or movie, do you go to the movies in the middle of the day, do you e-mail or are you on social media the entire day, do you play computer games and are you just not as productive as if someone was telling you what to do and when to do it?

So how do you schedule yourself? First consider how much time you want to work: 10 hours, 20 hours, 40 hours, 60 hours week, etc. Then divide up the day into work times and non-work times.

When do you go to work? When do you get off?

Remember there are some times when things have to fluctuate but we are talking big picture and not every unique day. Say you want to work 8:AM to 5:PM Monday through Friday. Buy a paper or electronic calendar that has each half and full hour. Are there things to put on your calendar that come up every week, once a month, quarterly, etc? Go ahead and mark them on the calendar as reoccurring. Decide how long your lunch is. Are you meeting someone each lunch hour? Give drive time to and from the meeting. The excuse I get the most for why people don't network or cold call is that they don't have time for it. It all requires discipline in how you structure your day. You need to leave time for networking, one-to-ones, cold calling, returning phone calls and e-mails, catching up and responding to social media accounts, marketing, administrative work and so on. There is plenty of time if you work out a plan and stick to it. Keep tweaking it until you have a solid schedule to follow. Make sure you put in time for picking up kids, walking the dog, going to the gym or any other daily activity that you want to make sure it happens each day.

You can increase sales and earning potential every day even if you are working full or part-time. Here is how I've maximized every working day to focus on the money-making activities during the day and during working hours so that I can grow my business:

Maximizing Earning Potential in 30 Days!

5-10 Hours Part Time

Maximize your Lunch Time:	Never Eat Alone!
Lunch Appointment:	5 Days - 3 New Appointments and 2 follow up/closing Appointments or Networking/Cold Calling Activity

1 to 2 hours each = 5 to 10 hours a week during lunch

10-20 Hours Part Time

Maximize Your Week:	Plan and Take Action!
Set One Day for:	Make Appointments/Follow-Up Phone Calls/E-mails/Cold Calling

2 to 4 Hours- Don't get Distracted/Stay Focused

Set One Day for: Networking or Event/Show/Conferences
2 to 4 Hours- Make sure you make those Appointments while you are there! It is much easier than following up later.

Set Three Days for: Appointments and One on Ones
2 to 4 Hours Each Day- Meet at Coffee Shops before or after Lunch and for Lunch. Remember to listen and schedule your follow up/closing meeting before you leave!

40 Hours Full Time

Pack it in! Give yourself 2 hours to do the appointment and get to the next meeting. Give yourself some extra time at networking groups to really network before and after.

Typical Day:
>8am to 5pm with 4 Meetings Set
>8am to 9:30am- Coffee/Breakfast Appointment
>10am to 11:30am- Coffee Appointment
>12 to 1:30pm- Lunch Appointment
>2pm to 3:30pm- Coffee Appointment
>4pm to 5pm- Follow up Phone Calls/E-Mails

Typical Networking Day
(Morning):
>8am to 5pm with Networking Meeting and 3 Meetings Set
>7am- Arrive at Networking Event: Start Introducing yourself
>7:30am to 8:30am - Networking Meeting
>8:30am to 9:30am- Stay, Network and Make Appointments
>10am to 11:30pm- Coffee Appointment
>12 to 1:30pm- Lunch Appointment
>2pm to 3:30pm- Coffee Appointment
>4pm to 5pm- Follow up Phone Calls/E-Mails

Typical Networking Day
(Lunch):
>8am to 5pm with Networking Meeting and 2 Appointments
>8am to 9:30am- Coffee/Breakfast Appointment
>10am to 11am- Follow up Phone Calls/E-Mails
>11am- Arrive at Networking Event: Introduce yourself
>Noon to 1pm- Networking Meeting
>1pm to 2pm- Stay, Network and Make Appointments (Last to Leave)
>2:30pm to 4pm- Coffee Appointment
>4pm to 5pm- Follow up Phone Calls/E-Mails

Typical Networking Day
(Evening Mixer):

> 8am to 8pm with Break in Afternoon and 4 Appointments
> with Evening Mixer/Networking Activity
> 8am to 9:30am- Coffee/Breakfast Appointment
> 10am to 11:30am- Coffee Appointment
> 12 to 1:30pm- Lunch Appointment
> 2pm to 3:30pm- Coffee Appointment
> 3:30pm to 6pm- Take Off/Freshen Up
> 6:30pm to 8pm- Mixer/ Networking Event

As you can see, there is time for appointments and they are not back-to- back without any time for driving, freshening up, getting yourself ready and leaving time in between for the miracles to happen. You have to stay focused and make sure that you fill your calendar with new appointments. If you have a time that is open, use it productively like making appointments for the next week. Don't just play solitaire or play on the web. Find ways to grow your business. Look for new opportunities. If you are at a coffee shop and you have a no-show or finished up early, who is sitting around you that you can start a conversation with? How exciting would that be to meet someone at random!

So this week, really look at your complete schedule and where can you improve? Where are you not maximizing your day and are you focusing on activities that won't generate you a referral or a new client? Be purposeful and your business will grow because when you focus on your business it is amazing how things progress! It is just like a seed, if you don't water it then it will always stay a seed.

Now, you have to take into account if you attend a function during the day or at night. Always be early and *stay late to any function* if possible. You want to be the first person people see and the last person they remember seeing. The actual meeting time is not the networking connecting time. Connecting time is always before or after the event. So, if the event is an hour and a half then you need to schedule in 2 and a half hours for it: half hour before and half hour after at least. I also give myself an hour and a half for clients and meetings. I refuse to meet with someone who doesn't want to give time to get to know me and vice versa.

Everyone has/had only 24 hours in a day… right? Donald Trump, Oprah Winfrey, the President, Ben Franklin, Thomas Edison, Helen Keller, the restaurant owner down the street, the pet at your feet. You are exactly the same.

Are you maxing out your experience on this planet?

Are you creating an existence that matters?

So, if you only have 24 hours, how are you using them?

Notes:

 # Chapter 4

"Life is too short to be wasted!"

Take a notebook with you for one week or at least a full day. Write down each time you change your activity even if it isn't that important to you. When do you wake up, what do you do next and for how long? Keep track of everything. You will be surprised how much time is filler time and how much time is not productive. There is always time you don't use. When you are driving in your car, what are you doing? People think it is weird that I don't usually have the radio on at all. I use the time to think. I contemplate and strategize the day, the week, the month, year, etc. I come up with great ideas, phrases, connections, and just a wonderful vision of something that needs to be tweaked or something completely new. I also listen to amazing professionals and experts to find new information and ideas from people who have already accomplished what I want to do. So what do you do when you are driving?

Another time that is usually wasted is breakfast, lunch and dinner. You should never eat alone. This is a great time to connect with someone, learn from someone, and experience someone's knowledge and energy. Networking groups, social events, chamber functions, open houses, grand openings, community activities and on and on are great for this. Take time and ask someone out for breakfast, coffee, lunch, coffee, dinner, and drinks. Just connect all day.

So now you are ready to schedule your day? What kind of presence do you project to the people you meet? One of the ways people assess your level of success is the stress level you project.

Do you feel and appear calm or are you in a rush and nervous?

Are you hurrying from one event to the next or are you giving yourself time?

Have you freshened up or do you come in to an appointment...
1. sweaty
2. wrinkled
3. unorganized
4. missing items
5. out of breath
6. late
7. rattled at missing an appointment
8. with cosmetics not on or face not shaven
9. damp from wet hair
10. driving a filthy car

If you said yes to any of these, the professional that people were expecting didn't show up. Now, we all have times that something happens and if one of these events happens then people will usually understand. Just apologize and move on but if they find that you are always like this, it will be hard to overcome their personal view of you.

One way to adjust so that this doesn't happen is simple time management. Have a good way to keep notes and appointment times. Give yourself plenty of time between meetings and don't try to do too much between each meeting. Arrive to every location 15 to 30 minutes EARLY. If you are there right at your appointment time you really are late because now you still must order your drink or food and you don't have time to freshen up. If you are there right at the appointment time, you also have no cushion for something that might go wrong: your last appointment went longer than expected, traffic was worse than usual, you had a flat, etc. and none of these should be an excuse for being late. Also, it tells the person you are meeting, if you are on time, that you respect them and their time. If you are running late, then it sets the tone as a negative right from the start.

I come from the old school of…

if you are 30 minutes before your appointment time you are early, 10 minutes before the appointment time you are on time and if you are on time you are late! So what label do we attach to you?

If you are "early" (15 to 30 minutes before the appointment) it gives you time to calm down and focus, freshen up, figure out what you want to order or grab your drink, find a great location to sit, have all your collateral materials ready and organized, anything forgotten in the car can be retrieved, etc. It also gives you the opportunity to catch up with yourself by returning phone calls, e-mails, texts, write down a couple of notes you want to focus on in your meeting or questions you want to make sure you ask so this "extra" time isn't wasted but productive.

Now go out and conquer the world! Make a difference in your life and someone else's you haven't even met yet!

 **Chapter 5**

"Business happens when a sale closes"

Follow Up

There are a lot of really hard adjustments for people when they get into business for themselves. One of them is the follow up. In the corporate world, usually there is someone you have assigned to do that for you or to at least help out with. Now it is all on you. It is extremely important to the success of your business. It tells someone that what you say is true. There are people who will test you to see if you do what you say you will do before they decide to do business with you.

My husband worked as a manager in an electronic store for a short time and sold TVs, computers, etc. It was right when the plasma TVs came out and each TV was selling for $10,000. A guy in his 60s pulled up to the store in a beat up pickup truck and was wearing some old blue jean overalls. He asked one of Michael's new sales reps if she could give him a quote for 10 of these TVs with a price break and to call him back at 2pm. At first the other managers brushed her off and wouldn't help her work up a quote. Michael and I always come from a place of plenty and never judge others so Michael jumped on it and helped her with the quote. The other managers laughed because they assumed that they were wasting time on someone they perceived didn't have any money. She called him exactly at 2pm with the quote. He told her that she was the only one who called him back and that he would have his assistant come over to pick them all up later that day to put in his two jets, and two vacation homes. Never assume and always follow up!

So when you follow up you are telling that person that they are important to your business and your business relationship. If someone sends you a referral and you never follow up on that referral, then that person probably won't send you another one. If a person said to call them in a week and you called them in three weeks, you may have missed the opportunity that they offered you. I always make notes in my schedule. If someone said to call them next Tuesday at 11AM, I would put it in my calendar as part of my schedule of appointments for that day. That way I would not forget. Most people don't have the memory space in their heads to remember to do something so figure out a way to remember.

It is also important to return phone calls or e-mails. Now, I know that you think this is an "of course" statement but there are a lot of people who procrastinate and never get to it. We all know what happens to e-mails if you don't respond quickly, they end up way down on your inbox or stuck in a folder that isn't read again. Voice-mail can be just as hard to follow up with if not done regularly. Make a time in your day that is your official follow-up time. Make sure it isn't during your busy money making time of the business day. Realize that most people have a favorite way to communicate. It is smart to find out from potential clients and alliances which way they like to communicate. So that way you know that they respond quickly to a phone call but won't return e-mails until late at night. This gives you information when trying to get hold of them or to get an answer to something.

Always be the professional, be in the moment. If the person you are with feels in any way that you are not there to really listen to them, then why would they care to build any type of business relationship or be a new client with you? Always take a minute and turn off your cell phone. Never text or look at your phone during a meeting. Immediately you have put everything and everyone at a higher importance than the person you are sitting in front of. Don't text back, don't read an e-mail, don't read a text, and don't answer a phone call. If you are waiting on someone to call to give an answer about something, then let the person know that up front. I'm waiting on a call from my kids, from the car repair guy, the doctor, etc.

Also, this applies to when you are in a networking group or large function. Be in the moment at all times. Nothing else should break your concentration at the meeting. Now you may be saying, "A new customer is more important than a networking group." You have to set parameters for yourself and for your clients as well. If they feel like you have the ability to drop everything you are doing to talk with them, then you will always have to drop whatever you are doing to talk with them. Most people understand that you are in a meeting and will call them back as soon as you are free.

Do you really want someone as a client that is so demanding that they want you to drop everything for them each time? I know I don't. I want patience in my clients. I want them to know that my world doesn't revolve only around one person and that I have a larger world reach than just them. Whatever experience you set up front will be the tone of the relationship from then on. Plus, if you are too reachable then what does that say about your business? Do you have nothing going on and is your business so slow that you can pick up the phone at any time of day or answer an e-mail at any time of day or night? But remember that you must follow up and not forget about that phone call or e-mail so that they realize that it is important to you.

I just signed up with a company because a gentleman had the best follow up skills I've ever seen. How could I not want to be around him more and learn his technique? He sold me that I was so important to him and that he wanted me to utilize his services so much that he wasn't going to take no for an answer. He was always kind but persistent. He would send me things when I asked, call me back, text me info, invite me to a meeting and he was brilliant at using almost every form of communication available. Most people LOVE feeling pampered and wanted!

 # Chapter 6

"Do not pretend you want to be the best in your industry when you want to work like an employee!"

Build alliances not competitors. This is very hard for most people to accept since we are raised to compete and not help those on opposite teams. When you find others who understand that the two of you have the exact target market and that not everyone is a fit for you then you suddenly find an amazing partner. Here is a gentleman who gave me a testimonial on this very topic:

> Before Your Local City, I would not be caught consorting with the "enemy" as I called them. Anyone that did the same thing in business as I did was viewed as a threat to me. Either they were trying to steal my customers or learn my secrets.
> Thanks to *Your Local City*, I've learn to embrace them as an ally rather than an enemy. There are several YLC members that do similar business as I do, and in some form or another have referred business my way; either it was something they could not handle or maybe a conflict of personalities. Nonetheless, the fact that they thought of me first means a lot to me.
>
> Now instead of turning a customer away because I don't sell the product they need, I refer them to one of my allies. My customer appreciated that I cared enough to refer them to a trusted business rather than just giving up, and guess what?... the world kept turning!
>
> *"Thank you Michael & Tonya for allowing me to see the difference for myself."* Ron Sauceda at the Color Factory *www.colorfactoryllc.com*

The hardest thing for people in business to do is to turn away business but once you reach that level you will find that you are now in business for yourself and that you are attracting exactly who you want to work with.

I know an amazing insurance gentleman. He has been an insurance agent for 25 years and knows the industry inside and out. He has a fantastic personality and is easy to refer business to. Now, you would think that I would send all of my referrals to him. While, he is usually in my top three people I refer to when I need to refer insurance, I do not refer to him every time. Why? Because he doesn't fit everyone and what is great is he not only knows that but doesn't want anyone that doesn't fit him. So who wouldn't I refer to him? For one thing, he has mounted animals all over his office so animal activists or anti gun types may not be particularly interested in his firm.

So if he had built an alliance with someone in another insurance company he could focus on his perfect client and send anyone else to someone he has confidence in to take care of that person.

Build integrity instead of desperation and most people will want to send business to you and end up doing business with you in the future. One incredible example is my building an alliance with my competition that ended up in the sale of my networking group organization to a national networking group organization. If I had not built an alliance with that person and only saw them as someone I needed to avoid, I would have never been able to start the conversation about interest in buying my groups.

I also love building alliances that believe in revenue sharing. I send someone to them and I get a cut of the sale. How great is that to help someone and still benefit.

So find those who can help you. Put together a group of people that come together once or twice a month to help send referrals and grow each others businesses. These teams will help you be around people who can bring something you are lacking to the table... and it can't be all about you. It should be a team

31

mentality. You have to bring something to the table but you don't have to worry how it will turn out just start it. Don't go too large. Start off with two people that you admire. Be prepared that you may outgrow the group or the group may outgrow you. Go find a new group. Who do you want to be like or who is really doing well in your industry or has a similar target market as you? That is who you ask.

When I started my company in 2005, I knew I had a long way to go. I joined networking groups and found a lot of amazing women who had the qualities I wanted to achieve. They were the networking queens of Austin. They would walk into the room and people would flock to them to say "Hi" and give a referral. They brightened the room with their presence and I wanted to learn their secrets. I was no one but I wanted to start a small alliance group to have the inside track to these incredible women. So I simply told each that I was starting a group and named off who I was inviting. I knew they all liked each other and they all said "Well, if _____ is in, then I'm in!" Suddenly I had five people helping me connect, learn, grow and experience everything that made them such winners.

Unfortunately, I found the sudden realty of my situation. I'm always on the move to grow and learn new things and most people are happy being stuck and too comfortable in the reality they created. After six months, I had learned everything I could and moved on past the group. Seven years later, two still have their businesses and still at the same level they were back then and the others went back to a regular job.

Chapter 7

"No business is complete without a smile and a true sense of confidence."

Professional vs Hobbyist

Most people have an idea in their head of what makes someone professional and what classifies them as just a hobbyist. The general belief out in society of what a professional is goes along with a career choice: Banker, Lawyer, Doctor, etc. and that a hobbyist is really anyone else especially anyone who is doing business from home.

My belief is completely different. My definition of what a professional is a person who is doing well in their career and who has a long-term commitment to building their business for the future. A hobbyist is someone who only wants to try it out and see if it works or someone who wants to sell or get out of their business or job as fast as possible. Commitment versus non-commitment is really the difference.

So let's take some examples. Jolie is a lady I know and is an amazing woman. You meet her and you want to know her. She is dressed professionally and wears a smile. She expresses her products in a well thought out presentation and talks about the future of her business. She is a Mary Kay lady and drives the ultimate pink Cadillac to market herself and her company. She showcases herself completely as a Mary Kay lady and when you are around her in public she is constantly expressing her excitement for her company and her product. Everything about her says professional. A lot of people knock her for selling lipstick but it provides her a great income and she is proud of her accomplishments. It hasn't been easy for her but she has succeeded where others failed.

On the other hand, there have been individuals who are in the "professional" arena who are farther from being professional than a lot of the newbies I know. Their hearts are not in the job or business they have, they whine about what is happening to them and they are looking for the BBD (Bigger, Better Deal). Who wants to work with that kind of person or send a referral to them? No one!

So here are some tips on creating a professional you:

Show Your Excitement

It is always refreshing when you talk to someone and their eyes glow and they express happiness about their product or service. When it is about what they want to achieve and not just what they want to sell you...the why is always more interesting than the what; the core beliefs than the item and the goals rather than the need. So figure out what is your why, core beliefs and goals and let everyone know.

The other day I was at a meeting where a lot of speakers come together to network. The room was full of triple "A" personalities to say the least. You would think that you would hear a lot of the same elevator pitches but this was farthest from the truth. They were there for different reasons. There were people who were excited about what they were speaking on, those who were very comfortable in their business and had lost some of their spark and those who were traditionally the whiners and they wondered why they couldn't get a speaking gig.

What I thought was really interesting is how people reacted to what I had to say. After talking with a gentleman about his amazing offerings, I told him about mine. He then told me "Wow, you have a real passion for your subject matter! You were so excited telling me about it." Now, I didn't go in prepared to wow people but it just happened. When you are genuine and really love what you are doing, people feel it! It pores out of you even when you don't know it. It also pores out of you in a negative way when you don't love what you do.

So what is your pitcher full of? Is it an elixir of happiness and excitement or is it sour, unsweetened lemonade? You can try and fake it but even if you pour a bag of sugar into your lemonade it will be just bad tasting lemonade. You really have to take on a new pitcher and start over. If you make the right mixture from the beginning, then there won't be anything that will get in your way!

Show Permanency

There are some simple ways that show if you are a long term investor in your business or just temporary. The old statement "it takes money to make money" still showcases the projection of people in businesses that are successful. You must not only show you are successful but also show that you are serious about being in business. Easy ways to show permanence are...

1. Get a name tag with a magnetic back and wear it. It is funny how something so small shows your invest in your company, your name is permanently etched in plastic or metal and can't be changed and you are proud of your company enough to showcase it on your chest.

2. Buy business cards from a printer. Don't print them off your home computer and don't get the free ones that advertise another company on the back. Temporary cards show temporary business.

3. Get a professional logo created for your company. Don't use clip art because you want your own identity. People notice when something is missing like a logo. You want everyone to know your business is really a professional company.

4. Create a company website and use an e-mail address with that URL. Get someone to help you if you can't do it yourself. If you are using Yahoo, gmail, etc. for your e-mail address not only are you advertising for those businesses and not yours it also has the perception that you don't have a real business. In today's business, you must have a website. It doesn't mean you have to spend a fortune but you do need one. Keep it simple and give information that people are looking for when they come to your website. It is about them and what they want: What's in it for them? Give them just enough to get them interested in talking with you further.

5. When you are meeting with a client, a possible business referral partner, a colleague or anyone connected to your business and you are meeting them for a coffee meeting, lunch or dinner make sure you order something. First it shows respect for the establishment that you are in and really it is a very affordable office space you are renting from the restaurant to do your business in. You want to show that you are doing well in business and can afford to buy a bottle of water, coffee, or something to eat. I know a gentleman that most people think of as very professional and always dresses very sharp. I referred someone to him the other day but they told me that they didn't think he was doing well in business because they never saw him order or drink anything at the networking group. So be aware of what messages you are giving about yourself.

6. If you join a "pay to play" type networking group, you are showing that you are not only able to spend money on marketing your business but that you are committed long term to build your business relationships with other professionals and want to build your sphere of influence.

Notes:

Chapter 8

"Don't wait… Challenge Yourself to Progress!"

Strategic:
Mentors, Coaching and Marketing for Growth

On average most businesses don't start turning a profit until the 3rd to 5th year that you are in business and some industries even longer. This is hard for most people to grasp. When someone starts up a company there are different reasons for doing so. One of the most common reasons is that someone sees someone else in business and thinks "I can do that and make all the money myself" but what they don't usually take in to account is how that person got started, how long have they been in business, how long did it take them to start becoming profitable or are they profitable?

Another one of my favorites is "I don't want to work so hard. I want to work for myself so I don't have to answer to anyone." Ok, so what does that really mean and is the statement true? My answer is that I don't know any entrepreneur that works less than what he/she used to and it just takes time to build a business. Time and money can seem to be your enemy. You have to ask, "am I willing to put in the time, commitment, money, sweat, marketing, personal development that it will take to be successful?" Obviously the answer for most people is no. That is why 80% of small business never makes it to the third year mark.

I always tell people that as soon as they get into business there are two areas that they need to focus on: Marketing and Coaching. You must market your company to bring in the clients to be successful. It has never worked by simply opening your doors to potential clients or turning on the "open" sign that will draw people in unless you spend a lot on an incredibly high traffic location. You must get out and network, put out ads, build your social media presence, build a functioning website, connect yourself all over the internet and connect out in the realm of your target market. People must know who you are and what you offer. Being a hermit doesn't work.

The other is coaching. To build a successful business you need to know up front what you don't know. Find the professionals who can coach you. My coaching clients often are amazed at the small things that make a huge difference in their business because the big things are just easier to see but the small things is what will tear down your business. Of course, how would you know what you don't know without finding out what you don't know?

Coaches are great also because they focus you on what is important. One thing that hurts most businesses is that you start focusing on working in your business rather than on your business. So it creates a condition of just plugging away on the day-to-day activities and never stopping to figure out what is wrong, what isn't working, needs tweaking, can be improved, or just needs some focus. Unfortunately, most business owners develop a "push me" mentality meaning that unless they have someone they are accountable to they don't accomplish anything. Don't rely on someone always pushing you. Take the initiative and get things done because you know you have to do it.

I meet a lot of people who want to launch their dream business, a book, a website, a practice or whatever it might be but never do because they are so focused on never having everything "Perfect." It is the perfect syndrome. I need to do this, this, this, this, this before I can do this, this, this, this…on and on and on. So you never have to get anything accomplished because it will never be ready. It is a very safe arena to be in. If you never launch it, you never have to leave your "secure" job or go out on a limb and have to promote your book or business. Safe, safe, safe… you never have to worry and if anyone ever asks you about it, you have a safe answer. I'm working on it. Just get it launched, finish the book, start the company or whatever it is just do it! Be uncomfortable, push yourself, and make a difference in someone's life by finishing your dream. My husband and I have an agreement. We aren't allowed to get comfortable! That way we are always growing, learning, exploring new things. And yes... of course there are times that I would LOVE to be comfortable but I may miss out on something truly amazing if I am. I only have one life and I don't want to wake up at my death bed and say "I wish I could have done more!"

Also don't wait for a pat on the back. You will have plenty of people tell you that you can't do it, won't finish it, can't start it, won't make a go of it, can't accomplish anything you set out to do, others have already tried and failed or you are competing against a huge identity and you can't make a dent. Get over it! Your family and friends will be the worst. Isolate yourself from the negativity. People love to bring down someone who is trying to be successful because they don't want to admit that they could do it too if they just had the kind of belief, determination, confidence and motivation that you have. I have only one main rule in my business: negative, mean and just plain grumpy people are not allowed! Wow, did that make a difference. I tell everyone at the beginning of every meeting, at every seminar and presentation, on my websites, etc. so that the rule is known, people stay away who are and I attract the right people that I want to be around.

We are trained at a very young age to be a follower and an employee. Most people are secure in this role. You have to want to be different which will cause you to be out of the norm. Most people are really followers and that is why the most popular question to you is "When are you going to get a REAL Job?" They really don't want you to succeed and not that they don't love you (family and friends) or that they don't like you (others) it is just simply that if you succeed when they believed in their soul that there was no way that you could then what was wrong with their beliefs. People are very self-centered. They take their own experiences and fears and project them onto everyone else.

I got comments that I would never make money dealing with small businesses over and over again. I finally had to stop and tell myself that I believe in small business and that I could make a living at it. You have to believe in yourself and your business, in your abilities and your purpose and in your professionalism and your commitment. With that kind of power it doesn't matter what you decide to do because no one will be able to stop you. And believe me they will try. You have to stop waiting for the pats on the back and the encouragement from those you love and admire. You have to stop achieving more only when someone gives you a "Great Job" or an award. You have to be able to give yourself those high fives and not judge your accomplishments by what others say or do.

- Are you always looking for self validation?
- Why?
- What will that change?
- What will that do for you?
- If you don't get it, will you continue?
- If you get negative slaps instead of positive pats on the back, will you still believe in your product, service, business or self?

Knowledge is one of those aspects that really is a challenge for most. There are so many facets of not only being in business but growing your business, your professionalism, your customer relations and your whole world. The best way to grow is to surround yourself with smarter people than yourself, find a mentor in your field and hire a personal and business coach to develop your business and your personal growth. If you had met me when I started my company and meet me now, you would not recognize me. I was an infant in my business and personal development.

Now most of the time we need a mentor and this may be a traditional mentor. Someone you call up or meet with and ask them to mentor you. This is great but be careful. This shouldn't cost you anything. If the person wants compensation for being your mentor, then that person is a coach or trainer not a mentor. A mentor should want to help you for the pure purpose of helping you. Who makes a great mentor? Try taking the person who is really successful in your industry out to lunch or dinner. Most people love the opportunity for a free lunch and to brag a little about how they have "made it." If the person is very reluctant to give out any info or suggestions, they won't be a good mentor. Go find someone else.

My favorite way to find a mentor is to study someone. When I began networking and was new to the whole concept, I studied those who were obviously successful at networking. How did they present themselves, talk to others, come in, leave, introduce themselves, follow up? I was amazed at two women. People scrambled to meet them, would smile when they introduced themselves, gave them hugs and energetic handshakes... I wanted to be those people. So find someone you want to be like and observe.

Be strategic in your approach to your transformation. How can you get the most out of who you are? That doesn't mean that you have to be someone you are not but be the best you can be. I couldn't be those other women but I could take what I saw myself doing and improve myself. What I liked, I re-created in myself. I could see myself doing certain things in the long run. I knew with a lot of work and pushing those comfort zones that I could be as good as or better than they were.

Notes:

Chapter 9

"If you don't care, no one will!"

How to Build a Referral Based Business

Commitment to Relationships

Being in business is a long term investment. The low hanging fruit (immediate sales) are great for the day-to-day activities and staying in business but they can not be the only way you do business because you won't be able to grow your business if you are only looking for the easy pickings. You must be willing to build business relationships with others that will send you referrals in the future so that it becomes a third party mechanism that is stronger than your first person selling. So let's take a networking group, there are 15 other business owners or sales reps in a networking group you attend regularly. First of all, just being in a networking group shows stability but also, those who see you wanting to connect and build a relationship with them that shows a long term commitment to your business. Building a networking relationship done right is a huge plus in your business because you now have 15 other professionals looking out for new clients and new business connections that will help your business grow and succeed. It is a very long term investment but well worth the time and commitment level. I had an amazing lady in my group who was an Aflac agent and she loved my company and was one of my biggest advocates. She decided to go a different direction and took a job and didn't need my services any longer. Three years later she sent me a referral and that referral ended up as an amazing new client.

Be a WE not a ME person

This really goes along with building business relationships because if you are a Me, Me, Me type person no one will send you referrals or even build a business relationship with you. No one even wants to be around a person like that. It shows desperation and isn't tactful at all. The scale always has to be full on both sides. You must give as much as you receive.

Did you thank those who gave to you?

Did you thank them for buying your product or service?

Are you keeping an eye and ear out for possible situations where you can refer someone?

If you never think of anyone else, why would anyone else think of you?

The questions I ask people if their statement to me is "Well, I used to network but I never got a referral"...

1. How many referrals did you give?
2. Is your industry harder for people to refer in that group?
3. Were you in a group where the target market of most of the people was the same as yours?
4. Did you ask people why you didn't get a referral from them? Ooooh .. that is a hard one! I don't expect most people to be able to do this one. You have to ask the right people to get an honest answer but if you can get that feedback, it really will be helpful. Some personalities must find groups that fit their personality.
5. Are you selling too much when you introduce yourself?
6. Are you trying to sell to the people in a networking group? No one likes to be sold to.
7. Do the people in your group really understand what you offer?
8. Have you been networking for longer than a year for once a month groups and longer than 6 months for weekly groups?
9. Did you have your coffee or lunch meeting with each member of that group? If you don't get to know each person than how will they ever be able to refer business to you or even care to? The only way to build a business relationship is to start by developing an actual relationship. Do you like the people in your

group? If not, they probably don't like you either and therefore won't send anyone to you.
10. Is it a leads group or a referral based group? When you give someone a lead it is "I know this lady across the street and here is her number." versus "I know a lady across the street and I talked to her about your product/service and she is excited to find out more!" That is the big difference... a cold call versus a warm or even hot third person introduction.

Some of you may have never heard of networking groups before. It can be a formal group like a city chamber of commerce or a networking group. It just means that a group of people get together regularly to build a relationship that will send referrals and give business support. Networking is really important. There are a few rules you need to make for yourself and the people you network with because they will be representing you through introductions. If you have a problem with them, their approach, their connections and their ethics then referrals they give will probably be like them. Do you want nice people, people with morals, a helper and a part of the community? Everyone looks for several different characteristics. I personally try to put myself around people who are positive, professional, kind, extremely well connected, love what they do, high ethics, on fundraising or nonprofit boards, and are always willing to have coffee or lunch regularly. You always have the option to quit a group. YES... you have the power to decide who you want to hang around and do business with. What a concept!

Chapter 10

"Torture yourself every day! Conquering your fears! It ends up being easier than your mind thinks it is!"

Recreating Yourself

There is a time in a very few, special people's life when they change. The change is into a person who has confidence and wants eyes and ears to be on them. Some are born with this gift. They are the true lucky few. Some find themselves and love who they see in front of them in pre-adolescence. There are those who blossom in Adolescence and others 20s, 30s, 40s, 50s, etc. And then there are most people who never find themselves because they are always searching for who they are instead of realizing that you have to create who you are! You have to be able to look in the mirror and really believe that you are fabulous and can say it out loud to not only yourself but to others.

I hope that one day you get to meet me if you haven't already. If you knew me in 2005 when I started my company (Your Local City, Inc.) you would have seen a very different person. In these pictures you can see the growth.

This is me in 2004 when I knew only family, a few friends and very few others. I stayed away from most people and only ventured out when all seemed pretty safe.

Wow, what a hairdo… what was I thinking! This is me in 2005 when I started Your Local City at the Leander Chamber of Commerce Holiday Party.

I'm cute but still not professional. This is in 2006, just after I started my first networking group in Round Rock, TX.

I'm getting there. This is in 2007.

Here I am on stage in front of 3,000 women winning the 2008 International eWomenNetwork's Business Matchmaker of the Year! I've come a long way baby!

Finally 2009, I feel like I have created the person I wanted to become. It was a long journey but well worth it.

2010, starting to speak at local events and groups.

2011, Sold my networking groups and started ramping up my national speaking career at Women's Conferences and Business Events.

2012,
The saga continues! Yippee… the book is done!

As you can see, the transformation grew along with the experiences and the growth of me as a person, as a business owner, as a networker and as a national identity. It also shows my growth as I grew from small town sales person, large town business owner, and national CEO. You can't expect to go from small town to national without a huge amount of knowledge and work.

My first step was to hire a coach to work on my beliefs and hire a coach to work with me on the business aspect. I was lucky because my husband had already gone through this transformation working in small to corporate environments. I had his knowledge of how to grow the company and the issues and problems he saw in the others he had worked in.

I have always been an introvert. I know… I've talked about this before but it was a major accomplishment in my life to transform so many negative feelings and beliefs and move past them. I appear to be very extraverted and love all the social aspect of networking and being around so many amazing people. It has been a true learning experience for me. When I was in High School, I would go all day without speaking to one person and no one speaking to me. As I entered college, I made a point to create an atmosphere of negativity around me so that I wouldn't have to interact with others. Why? I had a lot of issues as a child and was fearful of everyone especially men. I thought it would be easier to just keep people out than to have to deal with my fears.

I think that a lot of people feel this way. We love to take the easier way out. What started my change? I met Michael Hofmann when I was 21 yrs old. He saw something that he liked about me and he wasn't going to let me live in a bubble. He believed in me and I am so thankful. He showed me that not everyone is out to hurt me.

As I started *Your Local City, Inc.*, I had a lot of issues that I had to get over if I was going to be successful. I had fears that were debilitating and fears that kept me from being the entire person I wanted to be. In 2006, I took the whole year and worked on every fear I had. I reached the breaking point several times but I knew I had to push myself or be stuck and never able to change the world like I wanted to for small business owners. I had to figure out who I was and who I wanted to become.

So who are you? This can be a hard question to ask yourself. It is the most challenging of all questions because most of us see ourselves as no one special. Some people can't even handle fame because they keep the belief that other people are unique but that doesn't apply to them.

You see someone who is successful believes that they possess some special gift, talent, luck that you don't possess. The more I meet incredible individuals the more I realize that they are really normal people but that they have learned what it takes to be where they are. They have grown and overcome obstacles to become who they are. They have jumped out of their fears and moved past failures. This is all something that you can do too.

We all have fears and setbacks. The most successful people in the world fail on the average of 17 times before making it. Can you believe that? Sounds crazy but some failures are not huge and some failures are truly a step forward even though at the time it may be hard to see. Failure is only a learning experience in disguise. There are always people who are quick to put you down. Family and friends are the worst. They want to see you do well and be successful but they put their fears on you. When I started my company, people were very vocal about how I was crazy, going to fail, never going to get past the first year, in the wrong industry, targeting the wrong market, never would make money, could never go national, and on and on. Wow, their fears could have stopped me in my path. When it was really challenging in my business they seemed the loudest and it hurt the most. I had to finally tell myself that they didn't see what I saw. They didn't feel what I felt. They didn't have the passion and the reasoning that I had.

I knew why I was doing it. I knew what I wanted to accomplish and what my long term goals where. Of course, it was hard because I had to try different things and do a lot of tweaking before I accomplished it but that was fine with me. I didn't mind making small or even larger mistakes to learn something that would take me to a new level.

I had a fear of speaking because I thought my voice was not suitable. I had grown up being told to be seen and not heard even if no one said it in so many words. So I decided to create a radio show, a radio show that would air on the AM station to 25,000 listeners in Dallas, Austin and San Antonio! I was hoping that would help me get over a lot of the insecurities about my voice. Of course as soon as I announced my intention of going on air during a networking group, I had a woman come up and whisper to me that "You can't be on the radio... You have a horrible voice!" I have to admit it, I haven't cried in the bathroom since I was a teenager but her comment hit the very fear that I had right on the dot! Crazy, how people know what you are afraid of! Well, I did go through with the radio show. It aired in 3 huge cities and I had planned to have Michael's voice as the lead for radio show. However, the producer told me, "No, you need to be the lead voice since yours is more distinctive!" What a shock to me. What an eye opener it was for someone to see a positive in something I saw as a negative.

Chapter 11

"Enjoy the uncomfortable! Comfort and complacence is the slow death of a business!"

Rich and Famous

So do you want to be Famous and Rich? I usually get something along the lines of "I'm not in it for the money," "I don't want to be famous," "It isn't about me but my amazing product or service," and "I'm just in it to help others." It is hard to tell ourselves that we ARE special and that we deserve to be rich and famous.

Now understand when I say famous, I'm not talking Oprah famous. I'm talking about the people in your target market knowing who you are. This could be a small group of local individuals or a National branding with huge exposure. Each person has to decide where they want to go with their creation. If you want to be the best realtor in your neighborhood, then the people in the neighborhood must know who you are so they know to contact you to sell their home or to buy one in that neighborhood. You are famous in that realm of the city. People know who you are and must know who you are or they will never find you.

Also understand rich, you have to bring in money to stay in business. It takes money to market, promote, advertise and create an image that is sellable. So the more you bring in the more you can do. The more you do the more famous you become. Business is about spending money, time and energy to make a difference.

This has the tri-rule of money:
1. You can spend a lot of time and energy and not spend money,
2. You can spend a lot of money and time but not energy or
3. You can spend a lot of money and energy but not time

but you can never have all three at once.

When we start off our businesses, we usually have more time and energy than money and later on we realize that our time and energy is worth more than money and we change the way we do business.

Also, you need to know what the big picture is. Do you want to help one person a year? 10? 100? 1,000? This is important because this will tell you to what extent you need to create yourself. If you are a life coach and you want twelve clients a year that is one per month. If on the other hand, you want 120 clients a year then you need 10 clients a month. This is a huge difference in the way you approach your business and how you approach who you want to be. 12 clients a year lends itself to a more one-on-one atmosphere where 1,000 clients a year leans to more seminars and group coaching. If you want one client per hour and you want to work 35 hours a week, do you want to meet the person once a week, once a month, or once a year? That would give you 35 clients a year, 140 clients a year or 1680 clients a year. This will also give you answers to how to create yourself: locally, statewide or nationally.

When you dive into the question about how large you want to be you really have to be honest with yourself. It doesn't do you any good to push for a national exposure if you don't want to do presentations, webinars, group sessions, a comprehensive website, etc. Are you comfortable promoting yourself as a national expert? Are you always giving reference to someone else…"Joe Smith is so amazing and my work comes from his expertise" --that works for a small, local level. For a national presence you need to really create yourself and your product or service. "I started off as a student of Joe Smith and have developed my own beliefs and expertise in this arena. Now I'm the top expert in this field." This is a huge leap for most people. Joe Smith will always be "Superman" who has all the powers and abilities that you lack. I can't be Superman because Joe Smith is already Superman. What you have to understand is that Joe Smith thought someone else at one time was Superman until he created himself as a new, improved Superman.

So who is your Superman?

Who is in your industry that you can model yourself after?

Who can be a mentor for you? Mentors don't have to sit down with you and give you all their secrets. It is just someone you respect and you want to model yourself after. You can't be that person and nor do you want to. You want to be even better, bigger, more unique... You want your own super powers! The day will come when you meet someone and they look up at you with new eyes and say "You are my hero and I've always wanted to be like you." That will be a weird day indeed, when you have become a superhero. Yes, give yourself a superhero name. Even if you stay as a small, local expert, this day will still come because you will always grow and there will always be someone else who is starting from where you have started from.

Be a Super Hero!

Chapter 12

"If you aren't happy, your clients won't be happy!"

Positive Attitude

So what are some ways to "Create Yourself?" The one that has really made a huge difference for me is to realize that I have to create myself every morning. When I get out of bed, I do not look this good, sound this good, act with enthusiasm, etc. I have to create myself every morning. I put on the persona that I want to project all day. I find a nice outfit, do my hair and put on makeup to give myself the appearance I want to project all day. I snap on the smile and confidence I need to create the environment around me of people who I need to meet and influence. I fold around me the positive attitude that is imperative to make change and create a positive world and space that I want to live and work in. This all takes effort and a belief that I am this person. It uses a huge amount of energy creating, putting on, and wearing this persona all day long. Most days I have been "on" all day and by the time the evening comes around, I have very little energy left. That was a good day. I do have to remind myself that I have to leave a little for home, for the kids, to work out, and for myself but wow, what a difference it is when I have my persona on and when I don't. And often I have to schedule in a power nap. YEP... I said it! Naps are important especially for me if I'm out late that day.

One way to work on your persona is to figure out what you want to look like, how do you want to sound, how do you want to carry yourself, what do you want people to feel like when they are around you, what do you want them to think after you leave and will they remember you when you are gone? You see some people you know you don't want to be like. That person who is always slouching and not confident, sloppy and unprofessional, negative and unkind, a drain and unenergetic, unhelpful and rude, and you fill in the blank. Unfortunately we usually don't realize when we are one of these people.

We are usually the last person to know. I had a lady in my networking group who was incredibly negative and the world was always crashing down around her. She was nice and helpful but no one wanted to send a referral over to her or wanted to do business personally with her because she was so negative. So one day I did a program at my networking group on how we should be positive in business and especially in networking and building relationships. She came up to me and I was hopeful that it sunk in. She said that she was so glad that I did that discussion because she couldn't stand negative people! Wow... I had to tell her "This whole discussion was for you! I was talking about you because you are one of the most negative people that I know." She responded, "What! I'm one of the most positive people I know!" I didn't think I would ever see or hear from her again but that night, she e-mailed me. She thanked me for letting her know. She had no idea that she was ever negative and that it changed her life and the way she was going to approach people. I did see her the next week and she came in with a smile and a completely different attitude. What a difference for her, her business and those around her.

So how do you get out of a negative mind set? First of all you need to admit what you are negative about and change the way you think of it. I would pull up to the gas tank to fill up and be so negative about putting gas in. "Darn gas prices... always going up and I have to have it! How do they expect me to keep paying this rate?" Now I'm excited because that means that I went places, met people, grew my business, networked and went and did things that most people in the world never get to experience. I also was negative in traffic. I heard a wonderful talk about how we are not IN traffic but we ARE traffic! We are a part of traffic and part of the problem. It isn't done to us, we are doing it along with everyone else. It would drive me crazy when someone goes all the way to the point where you have to merge at the front instead of merging back at the end of the line. Now even though it might be nicer for that person to get in at the back, they are not breaking any laws. The law says that they must merge by a certain point. So now when someone squeezes in at the front, I laugh and give them plenty of room. I figure that I might make their day by letting them in with no problems and refuse to be ugly myself.

Another way is to take the mirror test. Now this is going to be easy for some and really hard for others! We grow up not believing that we are special and people are constantly telling us that we are not unique. Now, I want you to undo that. Have you ever really looked into your eyes before? Not to get out an eyelash but to really look into your pupils and then tell yourself out loud that you are Fabulous, Incredible, Amazing, Beautiful... etc. I was amazed how hard it was. All of the awful thoughts that swirl around in our own heads come out.

I'm beautiful... *"Well, if I changed this or got this fixed or not as pretty as so in so...."*
I'm fabulous... *"Well, if I was able to improve my speech, knew better words, was taller, was prettier, had a better speaking voice, was more like..."*

So now it is up to you to turn off the negative talk in your own head. We are usually harder on ourselves than we are on others. When it comes down to the real beliefs, it is usually our fears that are talking and not reality. There will always be someone who is better, prettier, smarter, kinder, more professional, etc. than you, so get over it. That doesn't make who you are any less valuable. All you need to focus on is making yourself the best you can be. A lot of times though we don't know how to accomplish that or even know that we need to fix something because we can't see it.

First of all be honest with yourself. People can see when you are faking it. Are you negative? Most of the time it is just our day-to-day attitude and we have become so accustom to being negative that we don't even realize it. What does it say about you? What are you projecting? I met a gentleman in Dallas at a networking group. At first, I was so impressed. He wore a suit and gave a great introduction about his business coaching company. He seemed to be successful and I was excited to help send referrals his way. Then I went up to him after the networking group to talk to him and get more information. This is when it all went wrong for him. I asked him if he was joining the networking group and his answer was all telling.

He said, "I haven't spent any money on my business yet and I'm just not doing that well yet to really start spending money on marketing."

OK, so this destroyed all hopes of ever getting a referral from me. You may be asking why? He was honest and probably could help people with their businesses and he was just a start up and needed the referrals to help his business grow. This is all true…however people want to do business with successful people. You must give off the impression that you are always doing well! When I give a referral, I want to know that not only will the person I'm sending be taken care of now but for a long time from now. Every new client should be a client for life! If I sense you may not be in business for a long time, I don't want to set up a referral to not be taken care of for a long time to come. So the old saying "Fake it until you make it" really does apply!

So, only focus on the positive! If you are new to an industry or business, don't tell people. They really don't want to know. If they ask, give what brought you into this industry and the skills you are bringing to the table. If you are new to a networking group, you don't have to say you are new. They all know you are new because they haven't seen you before there. If you don't know an answer, focus on finding out the information rather on that you just don't know the information.

Also, watch how you enter a room. Are you smiling? Smile and use those muscles often! It is harder for someone to ignore you or be ugly to you if you are smiling. Smile when you are on the phone because they can hear the difference. Give hand shakes or hugs generously. Listen to others and don't be a know it all. People do want to know what you know but they also want the opportunity to let you know what they know. You do not know everything so don't act like it! Give thanks and appreciations. Help others and they will help you.

Zig Ziglar said, "If you can dream it, then you can achieve it. You will get all you want in life if you help enough other people get what they want."

 # Chapter 13

"When fear has covered your eyes; You are blind to real opportunities!"

Get out of the Pity Zone: Victim Mentality!

What we have to realize is that we go through life with two options and only two: as a victim or as a creator. Are you only going to be reactive or are you going out everyday to make decisions and be proactive. Proactive sounds a lot better to me. First of all, realize that most people walk around with a victim mentality and never know it. Do you? Is it always... this person did this to me, this company took advantage of me, I didn't get any benefit from this, no one likes me, no one wants to do business with me, no one wants my service or product, I can't... I can't... I can't...

Is it always about you?

Is there someone in your industry that is doing fantastic? Then I hate to say it but it is you! One way to look at it is once you realize it you can change whatever is keeping you from being successful.

Really take a hard-look at yourself and ask... why is that person doing well and I'm not? Ask someone you have met and that will be honest with you what is wrong with you that people won't do business with you. Wow! This is very hard. It is very uncomfortable. I see people all the time who want to blame someone else, their clients, their products or services, the economy, their looks, their education, their mother, their children, the spouse, the moon... I could go on forever.

- What do you always blame?
- What is your favorite excuse?
- What is your pity card you throw out?

I know that life is hard...these things happened to me:
Rough Childhood
Cancer
Robbed and Tied Up
Molestation
Death of a Loved One
Screwed by Insurance
Divorced Parents
Struggling Financially

I kept a lot of these events as a crutch from moving forward; using these events as a reason for not talking to strangers, for not getting up in the mornings, for wanting to give up or just not to try new things.

So what about your life? It really is the mentality that we are never the issue or the problem. Understand that we all have a life to live and things happen. Focus on the good things and never the bad. How can we live in such a horrible world if the sky is blue and the sun warm, the birds are flying and hopping around looking for food, the peach so sweet and the carrot so crunchy, the ability to be mobile and to experience so much wonder? You must see the wonder in life! You are no longer the victim. So when you leave in the morning think of all these things, how are you going to be present for that day?

- Are you going to be happy or sad?
- Are you going to be negative or positive?
- Are you focusing on your positive traits or your negative ones?
- Are you listening to the clues that people are giving or are you going to ignore them again?

We always have the choice! Life is a choice and to be successful is a choice so make the right one. One of my friends is a quadriplegic and has very little mobility. She has a thriving practice and zooms around on her wheel chair with no fear. She is always happy. If she can be successful and enjoy life, than what do you have to complain about or excuses to give?

Notes:

 **Chapter 14**

"Your target market should reflect who you are because if not, they won't be your clients!"

Follow My Target Market!

"There is no one like you. There is no one who can be you. So, if you don't stand up and be who you can be then the world loses."

Perfect Client

So who is perfect for you? Now just because you limit who your target is doesn't mean that you won't take anyone else but it will help define who your perfect client is. When you know, it is easy for others to refer business to you.

Ask yourself...do you only want to work with...

1. Positive people or maybe unhappy people?
2. People who want to be educated or people who are already educated about your industry?
3. People who are struggling financially or people who have no problem coming up with the money?
4. White Collar or Blue Collar?
5. Men or Women?
6. A particular culture or industry? I know a financial advisor who got in with the pharmaceutical industry and most of his clients are pharmacists. Doesn't mean that he won't take anyone else but he found a niche that

works for him. It might be a certain culture you feel comfortable helping. There are a lot of businesses that focus on the Hispanic market or a particular market like the Women's market. This will help you define who you are comfortable with or enjoy working with.

7. A certain age group? This will be important especially in the way you communicate with them. Anyone under 30 is use to working off their phone and instant communication devices where someone in their retirement age may prefer to be contacted by phone still.

8. Those active in the community or solitary? You may want to help those who are out in the community and know a lot of people or maybe you prefer someone who can't get out of their home any longer.

9. People who *need* your product/service than people who *want* your product/service?

10. A part of town you enjoy working in? Do you mind driving downtown, to the country, or do you want to just stay 5 miles around your home/office? Know what your limits are and focus on that area.

11. Those at a certain education level? Very little education, high school, college, doctorate or even educated on a different level such as computer literate?

12. Technology skill versus Traditional? People who buy only on the internet or still read the newspaper?

One of the major questions to really analyze about yourself is who do you match and does that make sense for your industry. I met a lady once who decided to get out of the therapeutic massage industry and start up a mortgage company with a partner and focus on Multi-Millionaires buying a home. Now she was incredibly frustrated from the beginning... so what could she have done differently before getting into this situation? She could have taken someone out for lunch or dinner in the mortgage industry to find out some of the positive and negative things about the industry. She also really needed to assess her situation and reality. She dressed like a massage therapist not a luxury estate mortgage professional. She was in business for the first time as mortgage lender. Most people who are successful have grown up with the people they use, use professionals that they have built business relationships over their lifetime or asks someone in their sphere of influence who they use. So everyone should do some research in their business and into their ideal client before jumping into something that will not help your business grow. Also don't just look at the success of the top five percent, look at those who have been in a year, two years and five years to see what the norm is. If you are a normal type person then those experiences would be more informational than talking only to the top of the top.

Notes:

Chapter 15

"EVERYTHING is marketing! Everything you say, wear, send out, post, showcase and do! What are you marketing?"

Marketing vs. Branding vs. Advertising
How to Advertise to Produce Sales

Booths and Vendor Opportunities

An area that a lot of people jump into is a vendor opportunity at a local show or event. This usually means having a table to sell or promote your product/services at local events, conferences, community gatherings or festivals. This is a fantastic way to meet a lot of people in a short amount of time but unfortunately most businesses don't know how to make a really effective vendor presence and follow-up to get the most out of the experience.

Let's first discuss the opportunity. I always look at each opportunity strategically and realistically. When I go into any new situation, I'm looking for three new clients. Three is a very manageable amount. So when I had a 20x20 huge booth at the Texas Conference for Women which had a price tag of $5000, I still only looked for three new people. What I have learned is too really look at your ROI (Return on Investment). I can do a local high school spring show for $50 or a huge event for $5000 and still look for three people. What I have concluded is that it really isn't the event but will I have time to talk to each person who comes by.

You have to look at your business. If you are selling products, you want the 10,000 women event to sell as much as possible unless you can't afford to stock that amount of inventory. If you are a service industry or a "need to know each person" industry then you go for the "three" scenario. I must talk to the person to get some interest. Your approach may be to just get as many people on a newsletter as possible. In that case the huge events work. I also love "vendor shows." So what is a vendor show... in most people's eyes it is an unsuccessful event. That is when no one shows up for the event but the vendors. This is usually first time shows. I take this opportunity to talk to every vendor. They are my target market too. Build relationships with other vendors. They will give you information on other opportunities, may become a strategic partner or alliance partner or even may turn into an actual client! So as always maximize all opportunities!

The follow up skill is usually lacking in most cases when a business buys a vendor booth or sponsorship at an event or local show and then has no plan on how to contact those who are interested after the event. You go to an event and you have a drawing give-away. Now, who did you get to sign up for your giveaway? It isn't the booth with the most entries that wins, it is the booth who has the most qualified entries and then follow up with all of those entries and transforms the show connection into a sale wins!

So how do you make an impact at a show? I met with a gentleman who was going to a local real estate conference. He was so excited because it was a great target market for him. This is the first thing to ask: does this event draw your target market? So for him it was perfect and he was ready to find a huge connection to new potential clients. I was all on board when I was coaching him what to do and how to set up his booth until I heard what he was giving away. He was so impressed with himself because he had decided to give away a vacation to the Caribbean. I explained to him that this just wasn't a great way to approach this event. It is never about quantity but quality in the entries. I suggested that his give away should be one of his services.

He was concerned that he wouldn't have anyone enter but I encouraged him that if he only had one person enter that was better than 600. So what happens if you have 600 entries, you then have to follow up with 600 people who just wanted to go on a vacation and weren't interested in your product at all versus having five people enter and have to follow up with five people who have been qualified and will most likely turn into a real client.

600 people who entered to win the trip which takes five minutes to contact equals 3000 minutes which equals just around 50 hours! You probably will give up with all of the "No's" so you probably won't even find the five people who really were interested since they were lumped with everyone else! I always opt for the five people who really want to talk with me and spend those five hours closing all five. The gentleman had a drawing for one of his classes, had around 100 qualified entries which were 100 potential clients for him rather than 100 potential clients for a vacation. He was thrilled.

Have confidence in your product or service that it will be enough to draw people in and have them enter. If someone isn't interested enough to enter then you know they are not your target market. Move on! Also, make sure that you get everyone's e-mail address and have them check if they would like to get your newsletter! Even if you aren't ready to send out newsletters, start building a data base of people who are interested in you and your company.

Here are a few pointers for a great vendor experience:

1. Always wear a real name tag with your name easily legible and your logo, even if the event provides one. Never wear a handwritten sticker name tag that the event may provide. Be one step above the crowd!
2. Have a very easy to read postcard with great graphics for the attendees to walk away with. Have an offer but don't include an expiration date. They may not go through their items from the show for a while. All you want them to do is to call you at some point.
3. Only one business in a booth at a time. Focus and make an impact!
4. Have a great enticing giveaway. Make the forms to fill out easy to fill out! Have a check box for a few questions and make it simple bullet points. No paragraphs!

5. All purses, folders, cups, water bottles and personal effects must be stored out of sight. Keep a clean booth and keep out clutter. Be mindful of laptops and purses; they can be stolen!
6. The table(s) must be kept straightened and neat at all times. Professionalism is the goal!
7. Remember that you are a professional and if you have team members helping at the booth work as a team. We must respect each other. If someone approaches the booth, take turns greeting the guest and introducing them to your company. If a guest is talking to another team member, only give helpful comments or feedback when appropriate and never deliberately "steal" a guest that has already connected to another team member. Understand that shows and events are free flowing and that there may be several people that talk to one person throughout an event. There will always be people you connect too much faster than others and the same with the other team members. If someone really connects, you should always encourage that person to follow up with the lead. Just be respectful!
8. Make sure you put your initials or name on the back of the business card or sign up slip so that way the person can be entered in the drawing giveaway but you will know whose lead it is. Any additional notes you add on the back of the entry form will help you remember what the conversation was when you go to follow up. Include the following on the back:
   a. Your Name or initial
   b. "Y" – Very interested in following up.
   c. "N" - Not interested at all but just wanted to be entered into the drawing.

9. All leads with no initials or name should be divided evenly amongst the team members working the event. Initials can only be put on back if contact was actually generated with that guest.
10. Interact with everyone as they walk by the booth. Smile and always be courteous.
11. Booths are for Net "working" and not Net "sitting" or Net "eating" and especially not Net "Doing busy work or

personal chores." Always be ready for the next guest to walk up! You never know who that next person can be!

12. Dress professionally (no jeans!). As a professional you are representing your company and you should always be one step above your next client.

Events are exciting and very beneficial but are time consuming and exhausting. They can be very beneficial. Go in with a plan and a strategy on what to do there, what you want to accomplish and how to follow up afterward. All events can turn into a gold mine of opportunity. It all rests on you!

Notes:

 # Chapter 16

"Before you judge, discover the truth!"

Professional View:

So what is the reality of finding new clients? I know this fabulous lady who is in an MLM Company and she put an ad on the internet to find new prospects that might be interested in her business opportunity. The problem resulted when the information she posted for the opportunity was too broad. She got hundreds of leads and she was thrilled but then the realty of it sunk in. How was she going to filter through all of the leads? She thought about hiring someone to filter through them. I gave her a simple solution and one that is much more economical. Make the ad extremely specific.

Example: (Too Broad) Looking for people who want to have a business at home with flexible hours, unlimited earning potential and very little work.

(Better) Looking for one person in the Taylor, TX area that wants to work full time from home, has great follow up skills, can sell, wants to invest in your own business and loves to connect with people for this incredible business opportunity.

You will probably get a much better response and you will find someone you can really have a discussion with.

This really goes with business in general. Who cares if you are a realtor and there are 40 other realtors in a networking group. You want to stand out, stand up and be representative of the type of person you want to do business with. Niche yourself with the correct potential clients and make a statement on who you are looking for in a perfect client and no one will be confused on whom to send you for a good referral. So when you are doing an event, who cares if there are other "competitors" in the room. Remember... you want 5 not 595!

When I had just started my company, I didn't listen to my gut instinct not to take on this new person as a client and accepted her anyways. I didn't stand back and question the relationship and if I had I wouldn't have had a year long customer issue until her membership expired and I said good bye. She came into every conversation with a negative comment and I should have asked her what her expectations were going to be as a member of my company. What seems like a case of someone whose expectations are too high is really most of the time just a lack knowledge of your industry. What does that mean? I'll explain advertising and marketing later on in the book but this client didn't understand the basis of advertising and marketing and therefore had an expectation for my company that I could not deliver.

Presentation and appearance goes not only into how you look but every aspect of what people perceive you as. This is one of the easiest and hardest tasks to change and improve on. You really have to stop and ask some hard questions about yourself and get some real feedback. So let's start with your physical appearance. Do you fit the industry you are representing? Think about when you have met people and were surprised by their appearance when they told you what they did. Are you standing out from the others in your industry in a good or bad way?

Here are some examples: A gentleman I knew early on in my networking experience handed out business cards with his picture on it. He is a handsome man in his 40s and always dresses sharp. His picture was completely different since it didn't look like him and the picture made him look comical. He had on a striped shirt with a bow tie and he looked like he was at least 70 in the picture. I suggested that he change his picture. He took a new picture in a polo shirt and not only did it look like him but people could recognize him in the picture. He received numerous praises on his new picture.

We have all met someone who has a picture on their website, business card, flier, etc. that looks nothing like them. They have been Photoshop'd so much that they are unrecognizable or it is obviously a much younger picture of them.

You never want to use any picture that is a "better" picture of you than the real you. Now, YES... you can Photoshop a wrinkle or pimple out of the picture but do it only when necessary and only when it makes sense and doesn't take away from who you are. Too often I see people with pictures without their glasses or in clothes that they never wear. The purpose of a business picture is for someone to remember you and/or get a sense of who you are. When you don't give them a "real" picture of you, it is also saying that you are dishonest. If you don't want to show who you really are, is there something wrong with you, are you that insecure, or hiding something bigger?

So, who do you remember and how do you remember them? Is it the guy with the bald head who always wears a striped shirt or the lady with the large nose and pretty eyes? How do you think people remember you? If you are too plain or "normal" it will be harder. Make a connection to something so there is a reference that will spark a memory. For six months I had a husband and wife team that came to my networking group. They came late and left early and always sat in the back. In other words, I never got to know them. He was very tall and she was very normal but they were always a team. I ran into the wife at an event where I had a booth. She was there by herself and when I started talking with her, I didn't remember her at all. I invited her to my group and she was horrified that I didn't realize it was her.

If you run into someone who doesn't remember you, ask yourself why? Why weren't they able to remember you? If people can't remember you then it will be very hard to build a business relationship with them. They not only have to recognize you and remember you but they also have to remember you in a good way. There are plenty of people that will forever be in my memory as someone I don't want to do business with, don't want to refer and wish I could forget. Now you have to know that it is impossible to like everyone. That is what makes the grass green on both sides. Find those who you fit and you want to do business with.

Ten mistakes that people make and don't usually realize:
1. Mentioning and putting down your competition
2. Talking badly about your spouse or significant other
3. Telling jokes (it is bound to offend someone)

4. Discussing religion or politics
5. Being negative or a whiner
6. Always requiring the spot light
7. Having on a frown or serious face
8. (Ladies) Showing too much leg, cleavage or wearing tight outfits
9. (Smokers) Smoking just before you enter an event
10. Sitting down and not interacting

Here are ten ways someone can remember you:
1. Always smile and interact with those around you
2. Always be a giver, helper, referral source
3. Be excited about something you are doing
4. Talk positively about others
5. Be clean, smell good and appropriately dressed
6. Give others a chance to express their knowledge
7. Build alliances with others in your industry
8. Always shake a hand or give a hug
9. Be the first to congratulate someone
10. Encourage others around you

One of my favorite things to do is to encourage others. How many times in your life has someone told you that you are doing a great job? Most people can count the times on one hand if any. What does it take away from you to tell someone they are amazing? Nothing! You will always stick out as the one who believes in them. What a fantastic feeling that is!

I went to a book signing for a lady I have known for several years. She was so proud of her accomplishment and I wanted to make sure I was there to show my support and belief in her. She was taking questions and people were being very nice asking great questions about her book and her business. It was winding down and I raised my hand. She immediately put on a huge smile because she knew what kind of questions or statements I give. The anticipation was there on her face and I knew that I was a positive force in her life. I asked "So how does it feel to be this amazing?" With that the whole room of around 75 supporters cheered and roars of laughter and clapping hands rose around the book store. That is the kind of reaction you want. You want to always be a positive in people's lives.

So who have you affected in a positive way today?

Whose life can you change in a small way today by doing something kind?

Here is an exercise for you to do...go to a local coffee shop. Sit where you will see the most people coming and going. The best spot is by a napkin dispenser or trash can because each person will have to stop for a minute. As each person comes by, look up at them and smile. You can even add a compliment... Nice shoes, beautiful outside today, Chai tea is my favorite too, something to start a nice conversation. Feel the energy. Another exercise is when you go to a networking group, organization, church, school, whatever, do the same thing. What can you say that will put a smile on someone's face? Even a genuine, "It is so nice to see you today!"

Be genuine in whatever you say. People know when you don't mean it. Who do you like to be around? You may be someone who really does like hanging out with people who aren't doing so well or people who love to complain about things. If this is true you found your perfect niche. Whatever your niche is own it. Be involved completely and the more specific the niche the better. When you own it, everyone will know because your marketing will be clear and your message focused. You will appear more professional and it is easier for people to refer business to you.

Do you come off as having confidence in your business and industry? This is super easy to gain and to lose. Use the scale below to indicate how each statement applies to you. It is important to evaluate the statements honestly and without over-thinking your answers.

Assessment
(Mark below to indicate how each statement applies to you.)

3= Describes me exactly
2= Describes me sometimes
1= Does not describe me at all

_____1. I stand up every time it is my turn to speak in a group atmosphere

_____2. I give tone variance while I'm speaking so that I don't have a monotone voice

_____3. I can project to the back of the room so that everyone can hear me

_____4. I want to help others and I don't keep score

_____5. I'm always well groomed

_____6. I really listen to the person I'm talking with and ask questions

_____7. I never wear faded, torn, out of style or wrinkled clothing in front of my peers

_____8. I never lean on a chair or shift my weight on one leg when standing

_____9. I speak slowly and clearly

_____10. I have the right attitude to be the #1 person in America at what I do

_____11. I have conversations that are more about the other person than about me

_____12. I don't fidget with my hands or play with my hair or clothes when standing in front of a group

_____13. I have a happy and positive tone when I speak

_____14. I always wear a smile and ready with a hand shake

_____15. I look people in the eye when I'm talking

_____16. The tone of all my presentations and introductions are positive

_____17. I know I'm the best at what I do

_____18. I always try and find common interest or refer business to the person I'm talking to

Now fill in the scoring guide below from the numbers you gave each sentence. Then, add each box up to give you a total for that area and see in what subjects you are doing great and others where you need help.

Scoring Guide

Appearance	Posture
Statement 5 _____	Statement 1 _____
Statement 7 _____	Statement 8 _____
Statement 14 _____	Statement 12 _____
Total _____	Total _____
Speech	**Tone**
Statement 3 _____	Statement 2 _____
Statement 9 _____	Statement 13 _____
Statement 15 _____	Statement 16 _____
Total _____	Total _____
Conversation	**Attitude**
Statement 6 _____	Statement 4 _____
Statement 11 _____	Statement 10 _____
Statement 18 _____	Statement 17 _____
Total _____	Total _____

Each Box Score Total Equals the Scoring Below:
Scoring:
8-9 = You are on target in that area
6-7 = This area could be a problem
3-5 = You need help in this area

This is a great assessment to take several times a year.

Expert Corner by Gene Vasconi:

Communication in business and beyond:

In my book, "Say What?" I present what I call the "FIVE KNOWS" of message maximization. These are the elements that you consider as you compose any type of communication or make any type of contact. Some people call these elements "strategic communication" but the premise is the same: Think and plan before you speak or write.

Let me adjust a long-standing concept. Those of us in business are all marketers BUT...before we can even begin to hone that skill, we must first be communicators. So, you see my area comes first...NAH...NAH...SO THERE! Can I prove this? Well, if I must.

This is quite easy. In fact, I'll even remove this discussion from business and take it to grandma's house. You're ten year old is visiting...and she has a plate of those chocolate chip cookies! Oh yeah. I can eat about a million of those puppies. Now grandma walks over to you carrying the plate and says..."Betty, would you like some sauerkraut on your pickle?" "Uh...what? But grandma, my name is Johnnie and you're holding cookies? She's lost it ...I'm outta here!"

Grandma made her first mistake promoting her cookies...she didn't know her target audience and he got away. That is the first, basic concept of my "FIVE KNOWS" leading to maximizing your communication message. So, even before Grandma figures out the benefits and features of her product, she must know who her intended customer is in order to communicate effectively. This seems simple enough but these mistakes happen every day by people in business and even civilians who aren't entrepreneurs.

Everything communicates...everything. It doesn't matter if it is a hummingbird or a groundhog; a semi-truck or a helicopter. Everything has something to pass along to you – you just need to pay attention. So it is with people. We all have something to sell: Grandma and her cookies, the latest political candidate and his/her plan to save the country, the vitamin company and their solution to your "performance" problems and the list never ends. But, that's all OK because without these things we'd probably just be sitting on a sheet in the middle of a forest humming (with an empty stomach). So, it isn't the selling activity and even the profit to be made that can cause problems, it is when some folks try to do it and muck it up. Have you ever wondered why "Ethics and Communications" seem to go together when you see college learning courses? This is because they are inseparable. It matters not if you are a businessperson or other, you must maintain your personal ethics in any dealing. Your customers come to know your ethics as you deal with them but how do they discover them before that happens? Simple...by what you say and how you behave; how you communicate. Be what you say you are at all times and be successful.

Monumental amounts of communications impact us every day. That impacting is now at record levels compared to 50 years ago. We now have television, radio, newspapers, billboards, magazines, cell phones, I-pods, mp3 players, computers, Internet and every one of them is vying for your attention. Actually, THEY aren't vying...people are using them to get your attention. And therein lies the problem with today's crush of messages...it has becoming overwhelming.

We remain basic primates in our reflexes so we still lock into our surroundings for our own self-preservation. That means that you can relax in a field with no one or nothing around but when in a small room with ninety different activities going on, you get focused onto what is the nearest and most potentially impacting thing to your body. So, we become selective and soon filter out a lot of the clutter. We must in order to protect ourselves. This is why advertising and even one-on-one conversations can be challenging because people are just overly stimulated – they've closed down to so much stuff happening. Want proof? Easy.

I call myself a professional spy. That is because I've been in the TV and media business for a long time and have observed society mostly through the lens of a camera. This work has afforded me the ability to step back and observe and I do that even when having dinner.

Let's look at two types of dining experiences. A fast food place wants you in and out quickly so everything has a hard, sound reflective surface, music is fast-paced, and service is quick. It is all designed to get your energy level up high and motivate you to get out because they deal with numbers and not high quality. And I see you zoom in and out of there in exactly the manner they desire. They even provide you a drive through chute so you can snatch your parcel at an even quicker pace.

(Pause...take a breath) A fine restaurant wants you to linger and buy their best food plus beverages and desert and provides a softer, quieter decor. The music is soothing and lush; the food takes quality time to be delivered. You are being molded to relax, start to open up and receive their messages. To get you to leave they must shove a check in your face with a "no rush sir" so you will go.

Both establishments play to your reflexes as a primate and handle you according to their wishes. Success in restaurants and any endeavor (including your personal one) is all about knowing how to communicate to those you wish to convey your message to. Remember, communication first...then comes the marketing or networking.

One of the first rituals everyone must perform is to devise and refine an "elevator pitch." We call it that because it is supposed to be something you can present in a very short time while still being effective...kind of like you might do in an elevator if someone asks what you do. This is one of the preparatory items you need to create before you embark on any kind of networking or interpersonal activity because it is what tells your story. Everyone (and that means you too) must devise their elevator pitch. It doesn't matter if you are selling shoes door-to-door or seeking a better job. A properly crafted elevator pitch will make it happen or make it fail when encountering others. There are a few simple procedures to creating a superb elevator pitch. You will find them in my book!

So, communication comes before everything else. The little two-week old baby screaming his head off hasn't yet developed his elevator pitch but he still has something to say...diaper!!! He can't do much except communicate with his lungs. That's about as basic as you get so start there and re-think your style, your message, and always consider your target audience. Then go practice!

Gene Vasconi
Author, speaker, professional spy
www.genevasconi.com

Notes:

 **Chapter 17**

"Try walking forward with your feet facing backwards!
...I didn't think you would get far."

Getting Out of Your Fear Zone!

There is so much to fear. Most people can't even begin to think about starting their own business. The fear of not having a paycheck and knowing how much you can rely on each month is just too scary for most. However, a "real" job is never a guarantee. It is harder to fire yourself than your boss firing you. Not having benefits is another area. People love to argue with me that they have to stay working in a place they can't stand because they don't want to lose their benefits. I try to explain that they don't really get "free health insurance" but all they can see is that it isn't deducted from their pay check each month. Believe me that you do pay for your health insurance! There are plans that you can get on and pay it yourself and it should never be the reason for not starting the business you love!

We also grow up believing that "failure" is the worst thing that could ever happen to you. If you ask people who are extremely successful, they failed from 5 to 20 times before they succeeded but every time they failed they learned something that prepared them for their success now.

I personally love failing because I learn what didn't work and then what does work. It usually isn't a complete failure. It is all in the attitude! If you believe you can't afford to fail or won't be able to handle the failure, then absolutely you can't succeed! The fear of failure will keep you from taking chances that might be the exact attempt that will propel you into huge success! If the top person in any sport had quit if they lost a game or a challenge, then do you think they would be the top? NO! They have to learn from each game, from each match, from their competition, from the other team's coaches, from their coaches, from their team mates and more importantly from their own weaknesses and strengths.

When I started *Your Local City, Inc.* I had to find someone who would advertise with me when I didn't have any traffic and no one on my website. I also knew very few people who owned their own business. At that point and after a lot of "hell no's" I kept going and finally found someone who believed in my vision! Following that was the next onslaught of "no's" until I got my second "Yes!" I didn't give up. I kept going. I had people that would say incredibly ugly things to me. "You can't accomplish anything with this business." "You won't be successful." "You won't make it a year." That was in 2005 and I love that I was able to learn, grow and overcome all the obstacles that almost kept me from succeeding. Most people give up just before they are successful.

So let's go over some myths about owning your own business:

1. I won't have to work so hard. I don't know anyone who has had less work than having a JOB but the incredible pleasure and passion for what you do now makes up for any time you had before sitting in front of the TV. Now you just sit in front of the TV with your laptop answering e-mails at the same time. I truly love what I do and can't wait until each day to do it again!

2. I'll make so much more because the whole check is going into my bank account from my customer. Well, the truth is that when you own a business there are a lot of hands out waiting for most of that check. The taxes, the marketing, the brochures, the sales team, the insurance, the gas, the networking and the list is too long. It is true that you can make more than you can as an employee but most businesses don't make a profit for three to five years. You can't become successful and really achieve great wealth and prosperity if you can't push through the hard start up times.

3. I can just open up an office or a retail store and the clients will come. A few may come just by stumbling over you but

you will need a marketing budget. People must know who you are, how to find you, what you do, how you can help them, and having an open door and a working website just isn't going to do it. It is called work because you have to work. You have to hire marketing experts to figure out where your clients are and how to reach them. When my husband, Michael meets with people about how to drive traffic to their website, it is a strategic planning session. It is about who you are, what your business offers and the true benefit to a few amazing new clients.

4. I can do it all. Yes, at first you are CEO: Chief Everything Officer. Most people become overwhelmed from all the duties that they have to do to be in business. You have to be your Sales Rep, Administrator, Tax Expert, Technician, Janitor, and on and on. As soon as you can start figuring out what you are not good at or what takes up too much of your time to do what you love doing, hire that out. There are amazing VAs (Virtual Assistants) who can help with admin work on a as-needed basis, absolutely hire a CPA to figure out your taxes and build a game plan on what you can and can't write off on your taxes. You may not be able to close your sales but great at finding leads. Hire someone to close the sale. As soon as possible, hire those who will help you be successful.

5. I know everything about my industry or I can't afford to hire a coach. Even if you have worked in a very successful company and really know the in's and out's of that industry there are areas that you won't know. Usually the backend business issues that arise, legal, taxes, admin, or just being strategic on how to find new clients or develop your business. All successful people hire coaches. When you think you can see and figure it all out yourself is when your business stalls. Hire people who can look specifically at one area at a time and make those areas really strong.

6. I just need to do what everyone else does in my industry to be successful. You do have to figure out what makes you different from your competition. Why should someone come to you? What do you offer or how can you make your company stand out in your industry? Maybe it is just your personality or your experience level or you have different payment plans or... Never focus on the negatives

in your business: I'm brand new at this, I just started my company, I only can do this part time, I have this or that excuse. It will kill your business. If you are new, focus on how you love the industry you're in or what makes you passionate about it. People rarely ask questions about length of time unless you are showing signs of being new. Reassure them that you can help them in any way because you have people to turn to or you have been in their shoes.

There are many, many more but just the knowledge that this is going to be hard but worth it is the first step...that you can be successful but it will probably take time. You will need help and be ready to not get it right the first time. Grow, learn and ask for help. People usually want to help but they are just never asked. Even coaches will usually give you a free consultation to make sure that it works for you and for them. That way you can get a glimpse if you can work with them and if they can help you. Be ready to spend money... you are investing in your business, your life, your knowledge and more importantly your future.

I had to figure out how to set myself apart from my competition that came before me. The most resistance I heard about doing business with me was that they had done business with other website designers, other websites that sold advertising, joined other networking groups that all closed and they never saw the return on their investments. How could I show that I was serious about being in business and that I was not them? I had to really show that I was committed. I showed that I was hiring coaches, building alliances, did what I said I would do and sponsored local shows and events to set myself apart from others who wouldn't spend money on their business.

As we got bigger, we sponsored more shows and hired graphics professionals for logos and to assist with putting on my own shows and conferences. I tried new ideas and expanded my reach. Hired sales reps and hired new coaches in other areas we needed help in. These are all steps and you need to realize you can't go from "Newbie" to "Trump" status in one year. You have to step across the stream one rock at a time. Some rocks will be bigger than others and sometimes you will slip and end up a little or even fully drenched but you never have to go back to the bank where you started because you have left behind stones that you didn't slip on and wherever you start from you will start from there again. Be proud of those stones and don't compare yourself to others. There will always be people better than you at something and those who have already left behind the stone you are standing on but there are even more people still on the bank that will never make the first step. Be proud of yourself that you have started your journey and it is always OK to jump in the river and float for a while. That is why life vests were invented.

Ask for help, surround yourself with people who are on steps in front of you and do what it takes to be successful.

So how do you get out of your Fear Zone? In 2005, I was just trying to figure out what my business was going to be all about and if it was something that I could make money from. 2006 was my "get out of my own way" year! I sat down with myself and wrote down things that scared me... no terrified me! I had the normal "I'm afraid to talk to strangers," "I'm afraid to stand up and introduce myself at networking groups," "I am afraid of doing any type of presentation in front of a group of people." The first presentation that I did was in front of five women I knew and I thought I would die! Here were five very nice women who were very kind and why was I so afraid? It made no sense. I decided that I would start to attack each one of my fears because I knew that they were keeping me from succeeding. I knew I could be more than what I was.

I first found some mentors and invited them to meet me for breakfast twice a month. These were ladies that I was amazed with. They didn't know that they were my mentors but I wanted to learn how they did their magic. I wanted to pick brains and build relationships with them. It was fantastic. I learned that I could help them too, which was wild to me and they accepted. I also knew that I had to really push myself hard and I had to get over my insecurities. I hated standing in front of people.

Here is what I heard...
"Tonya, your teeth are horrible and your nose is too big."
"Tonya, your voice is shrieking and too loud."
"Tonya, what makes you think you know so much and why should anyone listen to you."

Well, I could go on and on. Of course, these were all in my own head. When I would ask my mentors about these things they looked at me puzzled because they didn't see any of the issues that I saw. I decided that I would start my own networking group so that I would have to get over being afraid of speaking in front of a group each week. I also had a hard time getting myself up and out of the house on Friday mornings so I scheduled it on that day. Now, don't get me wrong. I had plenty of people let me know that they didn't think it would work. I even had a guy schedule a competing group out of the people I was inviting to keep me from being successful so believe me when I say, there will be people who will try and stop your success but the only difference is that I didn't let them!

I launched my group and had between 20 to 80 people each week from that point on. Why? Why did it work with so many saying I was crazy? Because I believed it would and I found people who believed it would. Find people who will support you and encourage you. It is so important to find a group of amazing individuals who are a phone call away and a hand shake or hug for good measures. Make sure that you are as much a part of that group as anyone else and that you are their rock too. We all get tired of treading water and it is great to have a platform to jump on and rest sometimes. Who do you know that is a couple of steps ahead of you and/or is an incredibly positive influence? Be aware that ever so often you have to change groups. You will find that sometimes you end up passing up someone or they weren't actually at the level you thought they were on. Be OK with this. This is all on a flowing river. Nothing is ever constant. Be willing and open to change because it is a necessity in business.

Chapter 18

"Lions, tigers and strangers, Oh MY! Not too many people are that willing to eat your liver … so take the stranger."

Strangers Danger!

So most people have a hard time talking to strangers so how do you get over this? First of all you need to understand that if you don't let other people know about your amazing service or product then you are doing them a disservice. Why wouldn't you let everyone know what you offer and how will they know if you don't tell them? It is your duty to inform.

It is well known that you never eat alone and that you need to meet at least three new people a day. Get to know someone and invite someone to meet with you during at least breakfast and lunch. Then go to have a coffee break and meet someone there. My favorite is a local coffee shop. Why? Because my target market is business owners and sales reps and coffee shops are the office space for local entrepreneurs and sales professionals.

The trick is to start a conversation. Now you are probably saying… yeah, right! They are all in a conversation already with someone else or working on something. So you wait for an opportunity. The opportunity is small and quick so you need to be ready. I had an hour conversation the other day with a man who sneezed… "Bless you… looks like you are working hard over there on your computer. Are you a local business owner?" He wasn't but he ended up helping someone else I knew needed a job. Also, I don't bring up anything about me until they ask. They may not ask. Leave it. If you are coming in looking for a sale you lost already. Be a resource or a connector or just curious about what they do.

Here are lots of conversation starters and then continue with "Are you a Local Business Owner?" or whatever you want to start off with:

> Sneezing "Bless you...."
> A computer noise "Wow, what was that?"
> Seeing someone with a social media site open, "Would you like me to Follow You?"
> Unusual shoes or purse or anything they are wearing "Love your...."
> Someone obviously waiting for someone, "Looks like you are waiting for someone..."
> If you ever network at a Chamber, Organization or Networking Group, my favorite is, "Didn't I meet you at a local Networking Group?" You actually might have but it doesn't matter because these are all starting points.
> "Can you believe how hot it is?" The weather is always a great excuse to talk to someone!

If they don't want to carry on a conversation, it is ok. It is all a numbers game. I always offer to help them connect with someone else or to one of my networking groups that may help them in their business and usually, after some point of me talking about how I can help them, they turn to me and ask, "Who are you?" That opens it up for NOT a sales pitch but just an introduction. Leave the sales pitch for an actual appointment. Now saying that, I did strike up an amazing conversation with someone once that turned into a sale pitch because he was so intrigued and he signed up with me right there. So do be ready but don't expect anything.

Also, it is much harder to ignore you if you have a nice smile on and look very calm. No one wants to do business with anyone who is desperate for a sale but they do want to know who you are and how you can help them. Another tip is to talk loud in any environment that you are in. Again, it is an opportunity that someone else (and believe me when I say that people listen to other people's conversations) will hear what you have to say and want to talk to you. So say you are meeting for lunch to talk to someone about your product, service, job opportunity, non profit, etc. Sit some place in the restaurant where there are a lot of people around you. Then talk loud enough for at least the next table can hear you. I have had so many people talk to me after my appointment left. I never get up to leave right away if possible. You do have to give people a chance to say something to you. Too many times I want to talk to someone who I'm overhearing but they finish their conversation and off they go. Pause, look around and smile nicely at people and give them the opportunity to say something to you. Make it as easy as possible.

Listen in on other people's conversations. I had a fantastic conversation with a man looking for a job. I invited him to my networking groups and offered to connect him with everyone he needed to know since he was moving into the area. It ended up being his wife that he wanted to introduce me to because she was a realtor. She became a client.

Now, if you are still saying, "No way am I going to start talking with someone because they sneezed!" Ok, here is a great trick for you shy people out there. Go to a local print shop, office supply store or even some trophy shops will make a plastic badge around 1½ inch wide and 3 inches long that says "I talk to Strangers" or "Talk to Me-I want to know who You Are!" You can even set up a little homemade sign on your table at a local coffee shop that says "Please Talk to Me! I'm getting out of my fear of Strangers!" People love it when you are up front and honest about needing some help. Have a smile on your face and be approachable. If you look like you are sick, hurting, or negative, then it will be hard to strike up a conversation because people try and avoid those situations. You must be open to others even if you are scared.

Presentation fears are much harder. It really comes with practice. There are great organizations that work on just getting you up and talking. I push people to speak in front of the room even if they are super scared. Once you realize that no one booed you or called out ugly comments you start to realize that you can do this. I started listening to unedited recordings of professional speakers. What I found to my delight was that these amazing experts who get paid thousands and thousands of dollars say "Um," stutter, mix up their words, use the wrong word, and much more. If they do it, then when I do it I know that it is just a normal human experience. Not that you don't work on not saying "Um" or refining a presentation style but, when you do mess up, people really won't notice or remember.

We all do embarrassing things but what is funny is that no one will remember your flubs. I have way too many examples... food in my teeth, boogers, and spots on my clothes, "Ums," using a word that isn't really a word.

My favorite OMG moment for myself was in 2008. I was at the eWomenNetwork International Women's Conference with around 3000 women. I was nominated out of 25,000 women with 8 or so other fabulous women from around the world for their Business Matchmaker of the Year Award. I didn't prepare a speech because my self esteem still wasn't what it needed to be and I couldn't image that I would beat out these other amazing women. I have a tendency to not pay attention to details so when they gave my packet at check in, I failed to read the instructions to sit up at the front! So I sat in the far back of the huge ballroom with 3,000 women and they called out "Tonya...."

Well, my first reaction was "Wow, there was another Tonya." Yes I know... I needed a lot of help. When someone calls out my name when introducing me they always pause between my first name and last name. This is because their first reaction is to say Harding instead of Hofmann. So finally she finished with "Hofmann!" Suddenly I had more adrenaline in my body than I had ever had before. All I could think all the way up to the stage and up the stairs was "Don't Trip, don't trip, don't trip!" She handed me this beautiful glass award and took a picture on stage and then she said "Go over and say something."

Every fear I had swelled up and the adrenaline still hadn't subsided and I couldn't think of anything! I'm standing on the huge stage with all these people waiting for me to say something and what did I say?!!!

"I love microphones!" and as if that wasn't bad enough I finished up with "I want to have a one-on-one with every single one of you!"

Yes, not my proudest moment. I really beat myself up over that but what I started realizing was that not a single person remembered what I said that night. All they remembered was that I won and how excited I was. So remember that your embarrassments are usually only yours. People are very forgiving and their memory is about as bad as yours. So don't fret over the small things and only focus on the positive ones! Only focus on what wonderful things will happen to you today and never on the *should haves*, *could haves* or *wow, what was I thinking* moments in life. We all have them so move on.

So, list your fears and start checking them off. If you run into a fear, write it down so you can put it on your list. If possible, hit it head on at that moment. If you can't bring yourself to tackle it immediately, then challenge yourself next time. You have to push yourself each day to get over things.

Great quote from Dave Ramsey:

"If you want things you have never had, you have to do things you have never done."

That says it all! Just do it. No one else can make you do it or help push you to do it. The things to be accomplished must be accomplished by you, pushed by you and your self confidence will blossom!

How is your self confidence? Do you really believe you can accomplish anything or are you just giving yourself empty promises? I believe I can achieve the level of success I'm working towards. How much are you really working towards that goal each day?

Every Day: Work.
Not: "Oh today is too pretty to work, today is raining and too yucky to work, I'm too tired today to work," and on and on.

I used to stop on Friday mornings. I didn't have anything pertinent to get me out of the house and I usually wouldn't schedule anything at all or not until much later on Fridays. I was missing a whole day of work because I used the old… "The bed sure feels nice today and I'm really tired." So I scheduled my first networking group that I ran for Friday mornings to get my butt out of bed with no excuses. Now that is not to say that every Friday, I didn't curse myself when the alarm went off… "I could have slept in today!" but I got so much more accomplished with a full day of work! So get out of bed and enjoy life! Enjoy your business and all the new people you will meet and help today!

Notes:

Chapter 19

"Bullies, grumpies and meaner heads: You don't have to talk to them! Yippee!"

Avoid Toxic Clients and Find Your Perfect Client!

Who wants a customer who is nasty, unappreciative, and argumentative, doesn't listen, tells others negative things about you, takes up twice as much time, a whiner and/or mean? Now, if this is the way you are then you may be saying "yes" but if not you are like most people and you want to avoid them.

You move up into being a business professional when you can turn away people like these. Most new sales reps and business owners say "yes" to anyone who says "yes" to the sale. What you have to realize is that when you take on a customer, you want that person as your customer for life because it is always easier to keep existing clients than to go out and find new ones. So when you meet someone ask yourself... "Do you want this person to be with you FOREVER?" If the question doesn't have an immediate "Yes," wait and you will be thankful.

Now let me make sure you understand, there is a difference between a customer that is just having a bad experience and a customer who can't understand you because of a communication misunderstanding. Those who just didn't understand what you meant can be remedied by just explaining processes, expectations, or just rephrasing the misunderstanding. These can be your biggest and happiest clients because you took the time to figure things out. Those people that you can show your professionalism to are the ones that usually become your biggest advocate. However, I'm talking about the people that should have never become your client in the first place because they will never be satisfied.

So let's talk about Chocolate Chip Cookies! Just the mention of chocolate chip cookies has some of you drooling and wanting to run to the cookie jar to start a munch attack...or it did nothing for you. When I poll a room I usually get about half of the people who raise their hand as chocolate cookie fanatics! The others don't like them or are indifferent. I know... those of you who are having chocolate chip cookie cravings right now can't understand why there are people who aren't watching cookies jump around their brains right now.

This is the hardest concept to teach business owners. You don't sell what you like or focus on the part of your company that you think is important but on what your audience loves and desires. OK, back to the cookie story. Now, this gets tricky because most business professionals stop there. Yippee! I have half of the room I can sell to because they love chocolate chip cookies and I sell chocolate chip cookies. I had a coaching client that had this scenario. So, I asked her to bring some of her best cookies and give it to them. Afterward, I took a quick survey on what they thought of her cookie. What she found was only a quarter of those people said that they absolutely loved her cookie and wanted to know how to order more. She was heart broken because she thought that all the chocolate chip cookies lovers would be astounded by her recipe.

So what happened? Well, her cookie had walnuts in it so those who don't like walnuts or would prefer pecans didn't just love it. She also stuffed it with chocolate chips and half of the people just like a few chips in each cookie.

So how do you satisfy all of these different tastes? You simply don't! It is impossible. Instead focus on .5% of the population. What! Yes, a half of a percent! I know you want everyone. So let's think through this. How many people are in your target market area? Let's take Austin as an example. If you are an insurance agent, how many people can you realistically meet in a day? Say four a day which is roughly 80 in a work month. 80 a month equals 960 a year. Now most people can't turn a 100% closing rate on meeting with potential customers so let's take half of that which is roughly 500. OK, so 500 real clients a year. So if you take Austin which has around a million people in it, 10% is 10,000 people and 1% is 1,000 and .5% is 500. So, now you know that you have to find the half a percent that really are the best clients for you!

So, now you can focus on making the chocolate chip cookies that you love to make and your half of a percent will absolutely love and crave them! They will promote it to other people who are more likely the same type of chocolate chip cookie lovers as they are and will be your walking marketing department! Forget about the 99.5% of all the others who will either shrug and say it was an OK experience or say negative things. That half of a percent is much more fun to work with and will grow your business with solid love of your product or service.

This will help all of your marketing too. Now that you know exactly who to market to you will know how to market to them. Focus only what will make their mouths water to find out more! It will make a consistent message and a very strong committed message that will resonate with the half of a percent you are looking for.

So who do you like to work with? Make a list and be really honest with yourself. Think about what challenges you have with each group of people.

- Positive or Poor Me Attitude
- Age Group
- Economic Level
- Level of Education
- Culture/ Ethnicity
- Women or Men
- Introverts or Extroverts
- Industry base

- Urban or Suburbs or Country
- Small, Medium or Large Cities
- Employees, Entrepreneurs or Corporations
- Certain Group like Birders, Wrestling Fans, Roller Coaster Junkies, Grey Hound Rescue, A Non Profit
- What else really stands out for you?

Now put each answer together and POOF! You have your perfect client! So let's give examples. I know a guy who is in the financial advising business. He was really struggling trying to find EVERYONE! He told me that his wife is a pharmacist. I suggested that he start attending her gatherings where she socializes with other pharmacists. Suddenly his business took off. He had a common connection with a very specific group. He enjoyed this group of people and could really help them understand key areas of finance and became the expert that all of them began to use. They trusted him and his knowledge because he focused. They then would refer people to him and they often were very close to the same type of people. People are of habit. We usually hang around the same type of people we are because it is more comfortable. So when you find a group that really reacts positively to you then run with it! But first make the exploration on who or what this group is and how does it help you in your business.

Notes:

 # Bonus! Bonus! Bonus!
Daily exercises to strengthen your business!

So here is your daily dose of information, suggestions, development questions, things to think about, things to implement that day, reality of business, growth of yourself, beliefs that need to be challenged and ideas that could change your whole approach to what to do, how to market, where to grow and how to become incredibly successful! Enjoy each section and I recommend that you take this section of the book in small doses. Don't just read through the whole thing in an hour even though that is what we are trained to do. Read one or two sections and no more than four at a time so that you can go out and implement what you have read. This book is designed to be used, abused, written in, torn out and taken with you.

Each lesson has an idea for you to ponder, a story to help you understand each concept, a point to give clarity and an action plan to help you figure out what to do with this new information. Try and utilize one lesson a day and implement! Nothing will ever happen unless you make it happen! We skip Friday because who wants to do anything on Friday! But, read and apply on the days that work best for you! You will notice that some of the concepts are a repeat from the chapters. If you are anything like me, I have to have something get me to practice what I just read. So I included several in this exercise.

1st Section: Marketing

Monday
How to Target Your Market

Knowing your target market is incredibly important but rarely do we stop and reevaluate who is our PERFECT client! Here is an exercise to help you figure it out or reacquaint yourself with who you want to surround yourself with in your business.

Your Client(s)...

Men or women? _____
Employee or self employed? _____
Age range? _____
Do they live in the city, suburbs, country? _____
Education level? _____
Values education? _____
Single, married, divorced, widowed? _____
Kids, how many, age range? _____
Pets, what kind(s), how many? _____
Healthy, health issues, disabilities? _____
Nationality? _____
Religion? _____
Decision maker? _____
Ethical? _____
Mature or immature? _____
Invests financially or waits later in life? _____
Yearly income level? _____
Enjoying life or just getting by? _____
Own their home, rents, leases, on streets? _____
Great or poor self-esteem? _____

         And your target market may be other businesses. What
are some of their qualities you are looking for?

Product or service based? _____
Wholesale or retail? _____
Business to business or business to consumer? _____
How long in business? _____
Big business/government, medium or small business?
_____
Corporation or sole proprietor? _____
Home based, executive office or office space? _____
What part of the country or world? _____
Focus? Neighborhood, city, state, nation, global? _____
Created their own business, franchise owner, home based
representative? _____
Do they network? Where do they network? _____
How much do they gross each year? _____
Employees? How many? _____

Are they certified HUB or WBE? _____
Who do they buy from? _____
Do they sell on the web or just in person? _____
Here are some more things to think about to determine what kind of person really suites your business and your personality._____
What kind of lifestyle do they have? _____
Do they work all the time or play all the time? _____
What are their hobbies? _____
Are they sports fanatics? _____
Do they enjoy outdoors or do they do everything indoors? _____
Do they shop locally or online? _____
What kind of stores do they frequent? _____
Where do they get their information/news? _____
Are they last minute shoppers for gifts or buy all year long? _____
Do they stock up or buy as needed? _____
What do they care about? _____
Volunteer? Where? _____

Another thing to figure out is who do you love working with? What type of personality?

High energy, incredible networker, center of attention? _____
Decisive, gets things done, no non-sense? _____
Analytical, organized, low energy? _____
Caring, nurturing, fair? _____

All sound great but all come with some major difficulties too especially if you don't match that type of person. What type are you? Most people are in more than one area. Most of us have tendencies towards more than just one.

The **social person** wants to be the influencer. They want to have the attention on them and be rewarded constantly for their accomplishments. Their high energy also creates problems when things need to be done since they usually don't like to sit still long enough to get things done.

The **decisive person** really wants to drive and never be the follower. This is your leadership position but it is hard to ask them to let others be in the lime light. They also have no patience to wait and want everything done quickly. They also don't like to sit and participate so getting them into training is harder.

The **analytical person** is very detailed oriented. This is a fantastic quality until you need to get something completed since they are still trying to make it perfect. Perfection is their positive and negative in their business. They also aren't outgoing and have a difficulty with sales.

The **caring person** is amazing and holds the world's highest percentage of people but they are always happy with the status quo. They don't want to rock the boat and never want to upset people. They also avoid confrontation but are great mediators. They love to volunteer but rarely lead.

So where do you fall in? Who do you like hanging out with? Are they like you or are they opposite? Do you have a hard time with a particular group of people? If so, you want to avoid that group. It is always easier to work with those who you click with than trying to force someone that just won't connect. You know you are a real business owner when you can turn away sales. If the person doesn't fit, if you can't seem to get the message across, if you aren't seeing eye to eye then by all means find someone else to send that person to! Don't accept the sale because it will usually be more difficult, more time consuming and have the possibilities of ending badly than any other sale. You will find that the more you narrow your target, the easier your sales will be and the more your business will flourish. When you talk to the right people, you will surround yourself with those who love you, love your product/service and want to refer business over to you!

Tuesday
<u>Marketing to the Right People</u>

Idea: If you create a marketing campaign that talks to one type of people, every time that person reads, hear, see, experience your marketing then you have yourself a new client.

Story: Have you ever reacted positively or negatively to a commercial? I know I have. So much so that I have either supported the company by buying their product or service if I loved what they had to say or was appalled by it and refused to be a customer ever! For example: The Old Spice commercial with a handsome man riding a white horse who promised that even though my man couldn't look like him he could smell like him. So I went out and bought that bottle of soap. I was attracted to the silliness of it and its message. On the opposite end, any and all Jack in the Box commercials offend me. Even though they too are silly, the message doesn't resonate with me. I never eat there. What do you react to?

Points: Next time you see a commercial on TV or hear it on the radio and you think… "What were they thinking? I don't want that… or… I would never buy that… or… that was an awful commercial" then guess what, you are not their target market! So now when you experience a market piece that doesn't appeal to you, you simply state "I'm not their target market but someone out there is." If you say "Oooo, I want that" then what makes you experience that emotion? They have been able to talk to you as their exact target market.

Summary: Again, look at your Target Market list. Know that you aren't talking to everyone but those you do talk to, you will get a high reaction from them. Remember that those who don't get any reaction or a negative reaction aren't your target market and your perfect client and those who fall into your target market category will also be easier to sell to because they love your message.

Action Points: Look closely at your target market. What do they want to hear from you? What are they expecting? Find a small control group and see how they respond to your marketing. That way you will be sure that your message is getting across exactly what you want it to say to the right people every time.

Wednesday
Advertising vs. Marketing

Idea: Very few people understand the difference between advertising and marketing. I hear all the time "My advertising didn't work." What they really mean to say is "My marketing didn't work." Advertising is the vehicle in which you use your marketing to find new clients or get a message out.

Story: I know a lot of advertising companies and their owners. It is a huge frustration for them when they hear that, "My advertising didn't work." The advertising venues promise a certain distribution of its advertising. For example, a family magazine distributes 10,000 magazines to 10,000 families. So, yes the advertising did work. It got your ad in front of exactly what you signed up and paid for. What happens is your ad had very poor marketing! Remember your Target Market. Did you talk to them? Was the advertising venue the right one for you? Did you spend any time creating an ad that would wow your target market and get them so excited or want your product or service so bad that they would pick up the phone and call? Usually not. You just blamed the advertiser because you weren't talking to anyone in particular or even worse…to no one at all.

Points: Look at your Target Market list again. What do they want? Is your message compelling enough for a phone call? Are you choosing the right venue to advertise? Did you show it to a group of people to get their honest opinion?

Summary: You have to spend time on your business and especially marketing your business. Advertising is a great way to find new clients but don't throw your money at something if you aren't giving it a serious thought as to what you want out of it and more importantly, who do you want to react to it. Also, be realistic with the outcome.

Action Points: Ask the advertiser what the usual results are for most of their clients. Which ads have brought in the most new clients? See what the big guys are doing. If they have your same clientele in mind, what are they saying and doing to get a reaction?

Is it funny or serious?
Loud or soft?
Busy or simple?
Using Characters, Real People, Animated People, Animals, Babies, etc.
Old or Young?

Now you have a starting point to create an amazing marketing tool for your business.

Thursday
W I I FM Station

Idea: So you have been working on your marketing and who your target market is. Now you need to tune your radio station into the channel that every person on this planet has their dial set on for life... W I I FM or the What's In It For Me station. Without being tuned into that station, you are speaking to no one.

Story: There is a fantastic flooring company that I have bought from. The two gentlemen who represent the company are professional, positive and very knowledgeable. They would always introduce themselves as being prompt, bringing the showroom to you, customer service galore and very competitive on their pricing. None of this made me buy. It wasn't until they did a presentation and brought samples to a networking group that it hit my W I I FM. I touched it, smelled the new wood, and visually imagined it in my home and that is all that mattered. All of the other stuff is great and really expected but what did I want? New pretty floors! I'm a very visual person and I had to see it to picture it in my home. Now they always bring a sample to show people.

Points: What do your clients want versus what do they expect? What makes you different than other companies? Is it something that people really care about? Never assume what is important to you is important to them. You can even make a list of possibilities and have a potential client check off what he/she wants.

Summary: You may think it is selfish for people to think of only themselves but don't you? You don't buy something just because someone tells you to. You want it. What do your customers want? What do they expect and how are you going to talk to their want? Never ever assume you know. You must ask.

Action Points: Do you know what your clients want? Take a survey of your existing clients this week. It doesn't have to be a formal survey, just ask them. Ask potential new clients what they want. Only talk to their wants because nothing else matters and then you know even better how to market to them.

Monday
What Kind of Star?

Idea: What kind of star do you want to be in your business? Do you want to be a national star or maybe just a neighborhood star?

Story: When I meet with a client, the first thing I find out is how many people they want to help. They usually want to help the world. They want to grow their business so large that they really make a difference in a lot of people's lives. This leads me to the next question which usually gets an immediate reaction... "So you want to be rich and famous?" Almost always I get an answer of a solid "NO!" or at least, "well, being rich wouldn't be so bad but I'm not in it to get rich and I don't want to be famous." I quickly explain that we are not talking Oprah rich and famous but rather you must be rich to grow your business. People won't believe you are successful unless you are doing well and famous is just famous in your realm. The people that are in your industry know and respect you.

Points: So how did you answer the question? Did you have a similar reaction? So how rich and famous do you want to be? Well, take these factors into account: Do you want to be #1 in International, National, State, Metroplex, City, Neighborhood or maybe just #6, #100, or doesn't matter to you? Do you want to be Fantastic, Great, Good, OK?
What kind of star you want to be determines what kind of effort, time, energy, marketing, etc.it will take.

Summary: If you want to be #1 in the country and fantastic at what you do, you have a different way you have to market yourself, approach networking, connections and everything that you do compared to if you want to be #1and good in your neighborhood. The larger the area of influence the harder it is to market yourself and the closer you bring yourself to your local community the easier it is to target and market yourself.

Action Points: This week sit down with yourself and be honest and ask yourself how much money, time, effort, travel time, personal growth, coaching, experience, abilities, challenges and failures are you willing to go through to reach your goal? This will help you decide if being #25 in your city or in your industry is OK with you or do you have to be #5 in the nation.

Tuesday
<u>Successful and Growing</u>

Idea: To the outside world, do you appear as if you are successful and growing? This is incredibly important. No one wants to do business with someone that might not stay in business. If you sound and/or look like you are struggling, people will stay away. This is usually hard for people who just started their job or their business. You have to convince people that you will be around for a long time and that you aren't just trying it out. Too often, we give away signs that we aren't doing well or struggling to survive. Desperation comes across in a lot of forms.

Story: I met a gentleman at a networking group and we decided to meet for coffee. He worked at a local bank and I was actually interested in moving my accounts to a new location. He looked successful and had a great smile so I had no negative reaction that I wouldn't be interested in setting up a new account.

When he came to our meeting, he showed up late and gave an excuse that he was so busy because they had cut back people. This wasn't a great way to start because now I'm worried about the stability and functionality of the company. As we talked, he also expressed that he would love to find a new job or even start up a new business. I decided that this wasn't the stable environment I wanted to put my money. He never once tried to sell me on his company and working with him and instead he became a great client of mine.

Points: You can't be in business and expect people to just buy your product or service if you don't give them a feeling of stability. Most people buy from the person they like but they still won't buy or refer others to you if they feel like they won't get the long lasting support and customer service they desire. They want to know that you are taking this thing called business seriously. I tell my clients that there are two things that should be done first in any business: Marketing and Coaching and unfortunately it is usually the last two things that they do.

Summary: Do you have a marketing budget? It doesn't have to be a huge amount but you do need to market yourself. How else will people know who you are, what you have to offer and how fabulous your product or service is? You at least have taken the first step to business success: Coaching... through this book.

Action Points: When you meet people, what words are you using? Are you showing people that you are serious about being successful? Listen to what you tell people this week. Are you using words that gives people a feeling of security or stability or do you come across as being dispirit? Ask people that will be honest, do they think that you are success minded and growing your business or do they feel like you may go out of business any day now?

Wednesday
Appearances

Idea: Now I know, a lot of you think that this doesn't apply to you. You dress nice and you are always clean so why cover appearances. There is a lot more to what someone looks like than if they are clean and well dressed. What does your appearance say about you?

Story: Here are several examples of appearances that didn't work:

1st Story- There was a man who was a general contractor and built and remodeled homes. He would show up at a networking group in a full suit. It didn't fit well and the group was more business casual than suit and tie. In other words, he stuck out like a sore thumb.

2nd Story- I had a lady who wanted to sell me her line of cleaners, cosmetics and vitamins. Unfortunately, she showed up in blue jeans when I was in business casual, she wore no makeup and explained she couldn't wear the line and was complaining about being sick. Needless to say, I didn't buy anything from her.

3rd Story- I was waiting on a lady to find out about her services she offered and we had a meeting at 1PM at the local coffee shop. I'm there at 12:30 as usual. I've prepared my items I want to show her about my company, I've ordered and found a spot during a packed house at a table that I snatched as soon as I saw someone about to leave, I had freshened up and was ready. At 1:05 I called her to make sure she remembered or wasn't lost. She seemed irritated that I called since she was only about 10 minutes late. When she did arrive, she was flustered, wasn't prepared and forgot some items in the car, had to wait in line to get her drink and so it was close to 1:30 by the time we started. She gave lots of excuses, had a hard time composing herself and lost any chance of creating a new client that day. I, on the other hand, was ready and made the sale.

Points:
- ➢ Make sure you fit your surroundings and your peers.
- ➢ Always dress slightly better than your potential client.
- ➢ Whatever you are representing, make sure it fits who you are. If you are overweight and you are selling a weight loss product, let people know how excited you are and what it has done for you so far. If you are representing a product you can't use, don't focus on that item but rather on the products or services that you do use.
- ➢ If you are 10 minutes early you are on time, if you are on time you are late and if you are late, don't bother showing up.

Summary: I could go on and on with examples of appearances. It is extremely important. If you are a financial advisor and you don't look successful then why would someone want to trust you with their money? If you are a beauty consultant and your skin is always oily and filled with pimples then why would they want to try your product?

Action Points: How do you dress? Look at your wardrobe and ask yourself if you are dressed for success? Does your wardrobe match your personality and your position? Are you always flustered or calm? Make a point of being honest with yourself about what kind of person you need to appear to be so as you can be successful in the future. It is okay to fake it until you make it!

Thursday
Poor Me: How are You Marketing Your Image?

Idea: Haven't you heard it from friends and business acquaintances the traditional "Poor Me" mentality. Who likes hearing it…no one? This is incredibly damaging to you and your business. Never try to make someone feel sorry for your plight because they probably have it worse than you! Your image is a huge part of your personal marketing especially if you are marketing a local community.

Story: I was running one of my networking groups one sunny Friday morning and a new guest came in or I should say guests. It was a lady, her husband and a week old baby. The lady looked awful like a new mom looks without sleep. The new dad sat with the baby in a side table while the mom worked the networking group. I asked her after the meeting "Wow, you brought the baby." Her response was, "I was hoping that people would feel sorry for me and buy something from me today." She was totally serious and of course no one bought anything from her.

Points: Everyone wants to do business with professional and knowledgeable people. If people have even the slightest bit of a whiff of desperation, then they will avoid that person. We all want to do business with a company and a professional who will be there for a long time to take care of issues that might arise, for reorders, for support, etc. That is why confident people do well in business. We all gravitate to those who seem to have it all together.

Summary: So, what do you complain about? Your car and how you don't have the money to put new tires on it or get it fixed, how you want to go to an event or a networking group but are low on funds, how you know your business cards are wrong or missing something but you ordered 1000 and you don't want to waste them, how the postcards you are handing out say free from the printing company and are stock designs so everyone knows you go for the "free items" instead of spending money on your own design, or maybe that you don't want to have a "get to know you" meeting with a potential client or alliance partner because you can't afford all the expensive coffee.

Action Points: So examine this week how you talk to people. How often do you bring up a negative? If you are having a hard time, how many people know you are struggling? It isn't too late to turn that around. Always focus on what is positive in your business and your life. What do you talk about that shows growth? You can mention even that you are getting coaching through this book. Coaching shows a willingness to grow and expand your mind. What else... all week promote those things that you are successful at.

Monday
Free PR- Social Media

Idea: Ok, we are stepping into the Social Media realm since we have been talking about appearances and PR is all about appearances. So what is PR? Public Relations... fancy word for what do people know about you and what do they think. Before now, it has been hard for small businesses to play in this realm. Going through the traditional models of TV, radio and print was daunting. Now it is easier than ever and yes, that is through social media.

Story: When I started using social media like Twitter, Facebook, LinkedIn, I had no idea of the response that I would get from people. Every time I had a new member or a new leader join I would introduce them through my social media realm. Every time I would be nominated for an award or was going to an event that I sponsored, I would write about it in 140 characters or less.

Suddenly, even though I was doing about as much business I had previously been doing I had people come up to me and tell me "Wow, you are really expanding" or "You are really doing well!"

Points: People don't know how successful anyone is or not. Social Media finally gives us a way to tell the world what we are up to without spending a dime. People can see what you are up to. They can witness your growth, your successes, and your activities. Tell the world. Now I know there are some of you who are saying... "I just can't brag about myself." Get over it!!! You are in business. PR is a must for business growth. People want to see that you are doing well. So talk and congratulate yourself on each achievement even if it is small.

Summary: Grow your recognition to the people you want to know and to the people that already know you. What can you talk about that will accomplish this vital goal? How about which networking group you are going to today or tomorrow, what event are you going to or are having a booth in, new changes in your website, a new product or service you are now offering, new clients that you bring on board (you don't have to use names), something unique that you are doing for your business, a great new connection you made or something you did for someone else, absolutely any award or recognition, a coffee meeting you had and thank that person, and the list goes on and on.

Action Points: This week, get on line and each day write about something you did that day. Use the list that we just discussed if you need help. If you worked at all that day, there is something great to celebrate. Share, share, share and you will be amazed at the response. Get excited about your company but more importantly about yourself. You must self promote yourself because no one else will. Be amazed and in awe of what you did and can do!

Tuesday
Business Cards

Idea: Now you may think it is weird that we are talking about business cards but this is a huge point of debate in the business community because everyone has their preference of how they like business cards. Since we all have to have them, we need to cover the basics. So take out your business card and let's discuss.

Story: I went to an event in Houston and met a fantastic guy who wanted to connect. He also wanted to make sure that I put him in my e-mail distribution system to get reminders about upcoming networking events. When I went home to enter him in and contact him, I noticed he had no e-mail address on his business card. So he lost out in multiple ways.

Another story along those same lines is a lady who wanted me to contact her and I wanted to buy her product but when I went to my computer to e-mail her, I couldn't read her text. She had a dark back ground with black text and then the text was a calligraphy font. She never did get that order.

Points: The complaint that I get most from people about their e-mail address is that they don't want to be put on other company's e-mail newsletter "spam" list. So, my response is if you know someone and you give them your business card the e-mails from them are no longer spam. I have several times wanted to give an e-mail introduction and there was no e-mail on the business card. When you start your own e-mail newsletter, then you also have no right to send out anything to anyone. It is so easy to discount others and when you do they will also discount you. If too many e-mails are a breaking point to being in business, you really need to decide if you should be in business.

Another important point for all business cards is to make them legible! If someone can't read it then why bother. Pick a very simple to read font like Times New Roman or Arial and the size shouldn't be under 12. Look at your target audience, are they older? Then make the size even larger. Keep the colors simple. Put important information: Name, Phone number and e-mail address in black on a white background. Don't try to be too creative. It is just a way for someone to reach you!

Summary: Always try to keep things as simple as possible. What is a business card designed to do? Give them the information to reach you. Is it too much information? There shouldn't be a million choices on phone numbers... which one number do you want them to reach you at? Is all your information up to date? If not replace it and yes, throw away the old ones! It isn't wasting, it is all marketing! Are you telling people that it is more important to you to give out illegible or wrong information on a business card than it is to simply spend another $75 to replace it. Remember, those types of clues tell people how you are doing.

Action Points: So take your business card and really examine it. Ask around, ask people you know if they can read it with no problems, is all the information that they require on the card, are there any improvements that you could make?

Wednesday
Business Cards: Headshots

Idea: When you receive someone's business card it is important to know what your customers are doing with them. Many are going into a card scan system and are thrown away. Some people use them more for note taking so they flip it over and write something to remember that person by. A picture is a great way to help jot memories. Just make sure it is the right memory.

Story: I was at an open house and took a business card from the lady whose office I was at. She had her picture on it. It was a very nice picture but was either a picture of her when she was twenty or it was photo shopped too much because she was 65 and so the picture didn't look like her.

I was handed a business card from a guy who was a financial advisor and the picture didn't even look like him. He was wearing glasses in person and his hair color had changed and the picture had no glasses and different color hair. Both are examples of the confusion you create when someone can't recognize you. I get my picture taken every year because I know I have to keep up with my hair color and yes... even wrinkles!

Points: When people see something that doesn't seem right, it gives a sense of mistrust. You never want someone to second guess who you are. If you normally wear glasses no matter how much you hate them, they are who you are and you must wear them in the picture. Never do a glamour type shot that makes you over into someone no one would recognize. It is fun to do but not for a professional headshot. Make sure that the headshot is professional. You always want to represent your company as professionally as possible. Again it goes back to appearances and running your business as a hobby or as a business. Don't over Photoshop the image. Wrinkles and imperfections are how people know and love you. Don't hide them!

Summary: Pictures are great on business cards, marketing fliers, signs. It gives people a sense of who you are. So give them the person you want them to know. Give them the reality of who you are and not a perfected one. They want to know you and do business with you not an idealized person of you. Anything less than the real you is pointless to showcase but just make sure it is professional too. Also, statistics show that when there is a picture on a card, people don't throw them away. It also helps the person remember you.

Action Points: This week, if you don't have a professional headshot, get one! This is important on your website, your marketing items and everything you do. If it has been awhile and something about you has changed, then get a new headshot. Now you wear contacts or now you wear glasses. You once had long hair and now you have short hair. Get a new headshot! Do not stand against the wall and have your friend take it, get a professional one.

Thursday
Target Market Location

Idea: Now that you have your target market figured out and understand a little better about what is expected from your new clients and acquaintances let's talk about finding new clients. The most important item in your business is sales. Without sales you have no business. Even if you are a non-profit, the donations are sales and you must have them. So in order to make sales, you must meet a lot of people.

Story: One of my clients wanted to meet a lot of new moms. Her product targeted the first two years of an infant's life. She however was always running into people with five and six- year olds. We examined where she was trying to meet these new moms and she said the local neighborhood park. Now at first glance it was a good idea. She had a four-year old and it gave her an excuse to get out of the house and meet people but people who have tiny ones don't go to the park yet. We changed it up to find out where the new mom groups were hanging out and also at the grocery store in the baby aisle.

There is a fantastic connector that puts on events across the country and she wears a name badge that reads: I talk to Strangers. So guess what, strangers will talk to her. It is a brilliant marketing tool to make it easy for her to say hi to potential new clients.

Points: You have to figure out where you can meet potential new clients. Are you looking for other businesses to buy from you? Then networking groups and coffee shops are full of entrepreneurs. Are consumers your target? Health food stores if you are trying to find people who want to be healthy or gyms. The more you can hone in on where they are the more likely you can start a productive conversation.

Summary: Are you making it easy for someone to know you are in business and that you have a product for them? Wear a professionally made name tag. You can get them on line and have it clearly stated what company you are with or ask a question that will get a reaction. If people read it and don't have a reaction, move on! They aren't your target client.

Action Points: Get a name tag made. Keep it simple and make it super easy to read from a distance. You don't want someone to have to get up close to your chest to read it. So order one this week. I always order three: one for my purse, for the car and a back up. They do end up being washed because I leave them on jackets and shirts.

Next, figure out where your target market hangs out during the time of day you have open? Ask some of your past clients where they meet a lot of people that are like them. There might be a group that meets or a hidden gem that you wouldn't know about unless you asked.

Monday
<u>Why Network</u>

Idea: First of all realize that everything is networking. Whenever you meet someone new you are now connected and you have the opportunity to connect them to clients or to alliance partners and they can do the same for you. But traditional networking groups have come a long way. You have Chambers of Commerce, Associations, Organizations, Business Networking Groups, Women's Groups, and so on. There are so many opportunities to build a fantastic realm of connections. But why network in the first place? Most people believe networking is about getting referrals. This is a great bonus but referrals are not the end all reason. The truth is that if you look at incredibly successful people they are connected to one another. This is because they have learned the one rule in networking: Help others and help will come back to you!

Story: I personally know a whole lot of people across Texas and the country since I owned my own networking organization, went to so many events and other networking opportunities and speak at conferences and seminars. I have received referrals and sales from networking but it was things that I could not have asked for or paid for that really pushed me to believe in the power of networking. There is an amazing man who, while networking, I built a strong professional relationship with. I helped connect him, sent him key referrals that landed him some clients and helped him even further by giving him advice on putting on his own event. He was bringing in two huge speakers for his event and he asked me to be the only other presenter at his event. I was honored and floored.

Points: If you walk into a networking organization with your hand out, are you letting the people know that you are there to help them? Now you may be saying, I don't have any way that I can help people. I'm just starting my business or I've been inside my office for the last 20 years and don't know anyone. This doesn't matter because everyone meets new people each week. All you are doing is listening for opportunities where you can help them in their home or business life. It is amazing how many people don't ask for help when they need a connection. Create a spreadsheet with everyone's basic info which is easier to carry around than a business card holder notebook and make sure you include what they do so it is easy to give your friend, neighbor, doctor, hair dresser their info quickly.

Action Points: Find a group, association, Rotary, some place to attend at least once a month to once a week to start working on your connections. Even if you are nervous about meeting new people, once you meet them it is amazing how fast people are so willing to help and connect. Try it out and not just once, give it a real chance. Also be aware that it takes about 6 months to really be connected in a group so don't give up and always, always make your experience about the others and not yourself!

Tuesday
Who to ask for an in-person meeting

Idea: When you meet new people the most effective way for them to remember you and to be able to refer business to you is to have a one-to-one in-person meeting for coffee or lunch. This is a time to connect with the other person, find similarities and differences and figure out a game plan to build your business relationship. So, when you are first starting your networking endeavor, the best way to approach who to have a meeting with needs to be well defined to get the most out of each group.

I always look for four people to immediately have a meeting with. The first one is the leader. Once you get the leader to know who you are, the easier everyone else will accept you in the group. The second is someone who does what you do and is your competition! Yes, you want to know them and find out how you can work together versus work against each other. The third is someone who has the same target market as you. So if you are looking for stay at home moms and there is another person who is looking for the same this creates a great alliance. And the last is someone completely random! That is usually the best person since both of you are going into the meeting not expecting anything to happen so little miracles are more likely!

Story: This is always my approach in every event I attend. It has helped me from feeling scattered and overwhelmed since I have a game plan. So when I walk in, I identify the leader or at least the person that everyone wants to talk to. I know if I can walk into the next meeting and that person is happy to see me, then others will want to know who I am since I've been accepted by the main person. I talk around and only hand my business card to someone who asks for it. I know that I may get a lot of people who are interested in having one-to-ones with me to see if I'm interested in buying their products. Just a side note: Most people who network, don't network the right way so don't be offended if they never want to figure out how to help you. Still, make it about them! I ask if we can schedule a meeting after the event. This helps me find my other three people first before I start filling in dates with the other members. I try to meet everyone at the event if possible by having very short introductions and moving on. Take everyone's card so you can follow up with each person yourself.

Points: Always, always bring your calendar and be ready to fill in dates at the event. It is easier to make the appointments right then than follow up later. You can even walk into the room with four possible dates and times ready. Also figure out locations around where you are meeting to have your coffee or lunch meetings at so it looks like you are prepared!

Action Points: So, attend an event and go in with a game plan. Immediately identify the main person in the group and three other alliance opportunities. This will dramatically improve your results in the group quickly!

Wednesday
How to get more out of networking

Idea: I've heard time and time again: Networking doesn't work for me. It is usually the same story because people are just not informed correctly on how to make the most of your networking experience. First thing is that it takes time. You are actually building relationships. It is also how you are using your time. The

116

best results I have received have been when I arrived early or stayed late because the meeting is not the actual networking time!

Story: So I always arrive at least 30 minutes before the event. When I arrive early... guess who is there early... the leader, the VP, the ambassadors, etc. and these are the people who everyone wants to know and have a lot of pull in the group. They usually are not new to networking and have a huge database of people to connect you to! I'm always super helpful and always walk in with a smile and an attitude of how can I help you? The other people that always come early are new people. New people are great because they usually haven't been networking for a long time and need the help you can offer them.

Then I stay late to reconnect with the leaders because they are packing up and getting things settled and are who I want to get on the calendar. It is also a great time to work on your relationships because you can have great conversations when you give yourself time. I've even made important opportunities, deals and signed people up for a product or service by sticking around and talking. If you are always in a rush, you give off the appearance that the event and the people there are not worth giving the extra time.

Points: So arrive early and stay late! Put it on your calendar so you can accomplish this and you're not rushing out the door. Also, really connected groups usually hang around at the end to reconnect and catch up. If you are rushing out the door you may lose. There have been several times I wanted to give a referral or connect someone in the room to that person but they were gone and missed the opportunity. Slow down, enjoy and be present in everything you do!

Action Points: So mark on your calendars 30 minutes before and 30 minutes after each event. Arrive with a smile, calm, collected, refreshed (take a few minutes in the restroom to freshen up) and ready to tackle the networking opportunity that is a part of your strategic business model!

Thursday
Build Alliances

Idea: The best approach to networking is the idea of going in to build an alliance with someone. There are a lot of different names out there such as synergy partners, strategic partners, alliance partners but whatever you call it they all mean the same thing. It is an agreement with someone else that they will go about their day and after their sale is complete, when the opportunity arises or if they find a person who would be a perfect alliance partner for you that they will give that person your contact info! So in essence you have an extra free sales person, head hunter and scout keeping an eye out for your best interests. The kicker is always that you have to agree to do the same for them! So there are two main people you want to build an alliance with: Your competition and someone who has the same target market as you.

Story: I build relationships with other people who speak around the country at conferences and events. I keep an ear open for speaking opportunities that are looking for their expertise and in turn they look out for me. We let each other know about upcoming new events and ones that are searching for new talent at their conference. They also give me a great insight into an event that I might not want to attend because of whatever issue they may have had. I've found out and was accepted in to several events just by my alliance partner putting in the good word for me and vice versus.

I've also been able to sell my networking group organization because I built a great relationship with a national networking group organization. If I just had looked at this person and said "Well, she is my competition and I won't help her" then I wouldn't have been able to sell to them. You never know what lies around the bend.

Points: Your competition can be tricky since most still have the old way of doing business which is to try and shut that person out. It is a "lack" mentality instead of "the pie has no limit on slices." This could also be the person who buys your company from you in the long run so it is great to build a friendly relationship. Usually there is a particular clientele that you don't work with. That is a great referral for the other person. You will also find toxic clients that you cannot work with but they may get along great with the other company. Don't keep them for yourself... share the wealth!

It is very important once you figure out who your target market is to then figure out who has that same target market. So say you sell gorgeous clothing for women and when a lady mentions to her hair dresser that she is going to a fancy event in a month (you have built a great relationship with that hair dresser) he/she mentions you can help them with a new outfit. Or if you are a realtor and you built an alliance with a flooring guy, when he is putting in new floors because the home owner is thinking of selling his house that he connects the two of you. But remember that it has to work the other way too! If you are a realtor and you are listing a home for sale and the floors are hideous, that you give the home owner the flooring guys contact info.

Action Points: Do go and identify your competitors and those in your target market area and give them a call to set up a coffee meeting. If that person is really well known or has been in business longer than you and may have a great alliance built already with someone else, buy their lunch at a nice restaurant. It is amazing what can happen over a nice meal! Remember that the meeting is not about you... it is about them. Make them feel comfortable and then work out a way to help each other.

Monday
<u>Giving Always Comes Back</u>

Idea: Many believe that business is about making sales. This is true but when you are building your alliances and business relationships it also must be about giving. This is giving without the expectation of something in return. This is where most people flounder. They go into each situation with wanting something from everyone versus coming in with how can I help you today attitude. Just ask yourself if would you rather talk to someone who talks about "me" the whole time or asks you questions about you and seem generally interested in who you are and about your products/services?

Story: So you have heard me say that opportunities present themselves when I talk to others about their wants and needs. Once I was at a huge conference with about 1500 fabulous women. I was talking to a lady about what she did and she said that she wanted to get into events to speak more like the one we were at. I told her I would connect her to three event coordinators to put her hat in for their next conference. She then turned around and asked me how she could help me and asked for the same. She told me that she was putting on a huge women's conference in Las Vegas and she would love to have me there and speak. How easy was that!

Another time was at an event I was hosting with around 100 people in the room networking. A lady who was new to my organization came up very flustered. She told me "I was talking to that lady over there and I asked her what she did and she went on and on and on and then handed me her business card and walked off! She didn't even ask me what I do! You should kick her out because she was so rude!" So I explained that not everyone is up on the unspoken rules so don't blame them for not understanding the "It's my turn" rule. I also asked her if she offered to help that person in any way. Someone will stick around if they believe something will come out of it. She admitted that she did not and that she might have been looking a little eager for her chance to go.

Points: Next time you are talking to someone especially in a networking activity or even the person in front of you in line at the grocery store, stop and ask questions and then just listen. Can you help them? Can you connect them? What can you do to make their life a little better that day, next week or even next year? Don't mention what you do unless they ask! Don't start regurgitating your elevator pitch or go on and on about what you do. They didn't ask so don't let that screaming, crazy eyed, hungry sales person out of the bag! You have your name tag on anyways, so it is easy for them to see what you do. Do you have on your happy face? Are you smiling?

Action Points: So this week work on what can you offer people to help them out. It might be a sample you carry with you for a boost of energy, it might be a connection to someone you know, it could me an idea or an event that they should know about or an article you found. Figure out what you may be able to offer people and that way you will be set to be a giver than a taker!

Tuesday
<u>Elevator Pitch</u>

Idea: An elevator pitch is a short informative talk you give to someone who wants to know what you do. The reason behind the name is because if you are in an elevator and your perfect client or prospect is in the elevator with you, you have just a few seconds to intrigue them to want to talk to you further. Too many people think way too hard on this. It should be short and sweet and exactly to the point of what you do without being sales-ish.

Story: At a networking group, I met a lady who approached everyone at the group with one agenda; get someone to buy something that day at that event. People were laughing when she would approach someone without her knowing and people began to avoid talking to her. We then went over to a side table and she was in the group I was sitting with. She had a health product that was great and it had a product that helped boost energy naturally. Someone mentioned that they were going to need some energy later at this event and she immediately popped up with I've got the solution for you. She went on a little too long and then every time someone said something she would mention that she would be there all day to help them with their energy, or don't forget I will bring extra of my energy boost to help everyone. It was way over the top! Then when everyone went around and gave their elevator pitch in about 30 seconds, when it got to her she went on for around 5 minutes or more! No kidding... and yes, the leader of the group didn't stop her. She didn't get the too subtle hints from the leader, people starting to pull out their phones and text and checking e-mails, side conversations starting to go on (mostly about her) but she kept on going. After the meeting was over she again reminded people (as if they would forget by now) that she would have some products for them.

    She meant well, she was nervous, she hadn't been networking for very long and I'm sure we have all made these mistakes. Now you know to never make the same mistake she did!

Points: So what should an elevator pitch consist of? Your name, your company name, and then a very short description of one product, service or way you can help people and then follow at the end with who would be a great alliance partner and you can throw in a client you are looking for once in a while but it is way more effective if you ask for an alliance partner. Always take less than everyone else. People stop listening after about 10 to 15 seconds anyways so keep it short. Put some humor in it and make sure you stand up straight and yes stand up unless no one else is. Remember that the elevator pitch isn't to sell to the people in the room, it is just to remind them who you are and what you do. The one-to-ones are where they will really get to know what you do and who you are!

Action Points: So create a 15, 30, 45 and 60 second elevator pitch. Make it about the benefits of what you offer and not the specifics: Such as "I can help someone with the aches and pains of diabetes" versus "I have this clinically proven product that has helped thousands become healthy." When asking for a referral: ask for "I'm looking for a relative of yours that is about to go on insulin" instead of "I'm looking for anyone you know that has diabetes." Be as specific as possible!

Wednesday
Referrals versus Leads

Idea: So there are two ways you get connected to the 250 people that each person you network with knows. They will give you a referral or a lead. The difference is simple: a referral is to someone that they have actually talked to them about you and a lead is really a cold call but just that they saw an opportunity for you. Referrals are golden. It is almost a sure deal since the other person set the stage that you are the EXACT person they need to talk to about their problem, issue or something they want. A lead is great especially in the business to business realm because it might mean that you get a bid in before anyone else even knew about the opportunity.

Story: I've received both types. I get a lot of people who see an upcoming event and send me information about it. I can then follow up to see about being a sponsor but 99 times out of 100 their speakers list is already created because by then they are already advertising and marketing the event. The perfect referrals are from someone who knows the coordinator of the event and let's me know when they are still in the planning stages. This is incredible since I can also help that person from the beginning promote the event, give them any insights to other things I've seen done that works well at events and give them great leads to other great speakers!

Points: So what kind do you usually give? Is it a real connection to a warm body or is it calling up someone cold for a possible opportunity? What kind are you usually given? If you are in a networking type group, you may have found that you are in a leads group and not a referral group. If you feel like the people keep giving you a lead out of a phone book, then you may need to find a new group. Referral groups are very powerful but hard to find one that really seeks out referrals.

Action Points: So show by example. Give great referrals and try to limit how many cold leads you give. The more you develop relationships with the people in the group, the easier it will be for you to refer them. You will be able to remember who they are and what they do so that when the opportunity arises, you are ready to act. Never give a fake lead or referral! I know you wouldn't but there are those who do especially if feeling pressure from the group to give out a referral or lead. It is always uncomfortable to call someone who you think the connector already talk to and to find out that they aren't expecting your call at all. So don't do that to others. Treat others always with respect and the way they would like to be treated and they will give you that respect in return. If not, go find a new crowd to be around!

Thursday
Partner Networking

Idea: So many of you are just like me, I used to cringe at the idea of having to go to a networking meeting, mixer, event, conference, etc. by myself and talk to complete strangers! I found a simple way to help me get out there and say "Hi" without falling apart in the corner. For the extroverts out there, this works doubly good for you! Go to an event with a partner! Have them introduce you and you introduce the other person. Brilliant!!! You don't have to figure out how to talk about yourself and the other person will make you sound way better than you ever could.

Story: So I went to an event in Dallas with 3,000 attendees so needless to say, I was terrified! So many new faces, so many to meet, so many to have to approach... it was daunting! I invited a lady who loved what I did, had the same type of philosophy and had no problems talking to people. Solved!!! She went and approached people for me. I found that it was a lot easier to approach people and ask them if they knew her and then bring her over to meet them than to talk about myself. She would also bring people over to me to say "Hi." She never knew I had this issue but it just worked. By the end of the event, I was doing much better at talking to strangers that I ever thought possible!

I've work small events the same way. If I can find someone who is already part of that group, I ask them in advance to please introduce me around. They usually love doing that! Suddenly someone who is truly a part of that group connects you immediately in! It is so much fun working along side a partner at these events that you forget that you didn't want to go!

Points: So who do you know that is going to the same event that you can call or who you think may want to go to that event too? Talk to them about working the room together as a partner. If you have a group of people going to a huge event, get together before the event and make sure everyone has each others business cards. Also make sure that you know what the person wants you to say and what you want that person to keep an ear or eye out for! This also works for cold calling. If you hate cold calling, try it with a group of people or with one more person not in your same industry. I've done this and it is a lot of fun to walk into a store with four smiling faces, introducing everyone to the person behind the counter and seeing how we can fit a need for that person! Now you are having fun! Get the extrovert or the person great at introducing the group to talk first!

Action Points: So find your partner, devise a plan, be strategic, know what to say, be ready and go for it! It will be the easiest networking you have ever done!

Monday
<u>One-to-Ones</u>

Idea: One-to-ones are incredibly important. This is your lunch or coffee in-person meeting. Most people have an opinion about how effective they are and if they should sell during the meeting or not. The answer is that most people won't remember you and won't refer business to you until they get to know you. They can do that by just coming to a networking group but that takes a long time. A one-to-one really speeds up that process but you don't want to ever have a bad experience at one or nothing will happen in the future.

Story: I've had incredibly long one-to-ones and amazingly short ones. The ones I enjoy the most have two basic components: a personal and a business information section. When I book a one-to-one I lay out the ground work for what I expect to happen. "I want to find out more about you and really understand your business and give you information about who I am and what my business is all about." This is important to lay out the "If we meet, you have to listen to me too!" I always let them go first and then it is my turn.

I've got so many examples it could fill a book. My favorite is when I met with another business coach. She specialized in social media and even though I touched on it briefly I didn't go into all the how's and why's. We first talked about kids, where we lived, background info and then she went into her business and I went into mine. We then figured out exactly how we were going to play in each others realms. Who we could send as a referral, who and what to look out for as an alliance partner and so by the time we walked away we knew exactly how to proceed with our relationship. It has been an incredibly productive alliance with many returns on my hour investment of time.

Points: So set the stage when you book the appointment. What do you want to happen? Do you want to show them your products and services? Are you showing it to them so they will buy or so they will be able to go out and refer people to you? If you are only there to sell them then they will know and the meeting is over. Be there to really want to build a mutually beneficial relationship! It is amazing how some people always expect a referral or a sale when they aren't willing to do the same in return. If you are interested in buying their product or service then that is great but don't expect them to buy in return. I hear way too often people that want to support the others in the group but then get upset when no one buys their items.

Action Points: So this week, build relationships and ask for one-to-ones. Give a clear outline of what you expect to happen. You will be amazed how much you increase your referrals and sales when you make it a clear and precise meeting for both of you. Develop a plan with the other person on how both of you can walk away and help each other that week. The more specific and the clearer the plan the easier it becomes to see the opportunities out there for both of you!

Tuesday
Speak Loud in a Loud Room

Idea: I'm always amazed that people want to go some place quiet and vacant to work. Now there are times when you need a little less noise but most of the time during the day, you can bring your laptop and plop down to check e-mails before heading home. Also for one-to-ones or client meetings (unless it is a confidential meeting) go some place busy so in that way people are there to listen to you. Yes… you want people to eavesdrop. Why wouldn't you? You basically can have two presentations or more for the price of one!

Story: I always pick the empty table in the middle of the action and talk as loud as possible without the other side of the restaurant hearing me. I schedule all my meetings that aren't my coaching clients at incredibly busy coffee shops. For example, I was at a packed coffee shop and was giving a presentation to a potential new client. After we were done and after I signed up the new client, I hung around for a few minutes since I never try and rush out. Thank goodness I didn't because I guy who had his back to me in the next table turned around and started asking me some questions since he was listening in. He signed up before I left! He had heard my presentation and wanted it too!

One of my favorite clients told me that he was at a meeting where he was being interviewed by a potential new client that wanted to know more about what he specialized in and his knowledge in the industry. When his meeting was over and his new client left, he was gathering his things and a guy who was sitting next to his table had overheard the interview and asked him more about what he did. The stranger ended up being the largest client he ever had!

Points: The point is that you just don't know who is sitting around you and if they may be interested or not. If you whisper and sit way off to the side or back, then you would absolutely guarantee that nothing will ever happen! If you speak up a little and show your passion and excitement for what you do, that will translate far beyond the person sitting in front of you.

Action Points: So for the rest of this week and the month, every meeting you have... you have already scheduled to arrive a little early so go ahead and make sure that the hostess seats you or you seat yourself in the middle of the action where there are close tables to all sides of you. Position yourself so that your voice will be projecting out towards the room and not towards a wall or window so that more people will be able to hear you. Put out your business card, folder or something that has your logo or product/service on it so that it is easy for others around you to see what you do and who you are connected to. Give people the opportunity to say "Hi" and make you more approachable. Be ready for anything to happen!

Wednesday
Remembering You

Idea: The hardest thing to accomplish in your business is to get people to remember who you are and have them connect with you for a new product/service they need, when they are ready to buy, to see a referral opportunity and to see something that would benefit you. Most people on the average know 250 people. So how are you going to make an impact on that person's memory to recall who you are, your name, what your product or service does and how to get a hold of you? Most people never stand out in any way or create a trigger point so that someone will think of you when the time is right.

Story: Most one-to-ones I forget quickly. I meet around 250 people a week and especially at events where I'm looking at 500 faces or more and they are all looking at only me I have a distinct disadvantage when it comes to remembering each of them. Most people don't have as many to remember but even then it can be difficult. Stories are memorable! People will remember stories before anything else and the more you can tie it to your product or service the better.

There is a lady in Dallas who goes to a women's networking group. She wears red shoes all the time and has coined herself the red shoe lady. She sells real estate and she has a nice saying about how she keeps her feet on fire from all the homes she puts people into so that is why they are red. I've only met this woman once but I still remember her. A presentation you are giving or the one-to-one you are having will not have an impact unless you tie it to a story.

Points: So think of what kind of stories you can tell. Where are you from, what are your hobbies, is there something you love to eat, play, create that you can tie to your elevator pitch, your presentations, your business? You must come up with some great reason you are in business, why you love your product or service, something that has changed your life or someone close to you. The stories must be personal and meaningful. They are truthful and passionate. They make an impact on the group or person when you give it. If someone ever mentioned a story you told them a while back, that is the perfect one to tell again. What makes you unique and creates a memory in someone else's mind?

Action Points: So this week, sit down and think of all the stories you can pull from. Eliminate any that aren't personal stories to you. Can any of the stories be tied into your business? Is there a hobby or passion that sets you a part that you can use as a story line and theme of your elevator pitch, presentations and throughout your marketing? Make this change in your presentations and you will increase the memory factor in all who come into contact with you!

Section 2: Personal Development

As a reminder, each lesson has an idea for you to ponder, a story to help you understand each concept, a point to give clarity and an action plan to help you figure out what to do with this new information. Try and utilize one lesson a day and implement it! Nothing will ever happen unless you make it happen! We skip Friday because who wants to do anything on Friday! But, read and apply on the days that work best for you! You will notice that some of the concepts are a repeat from the chapters. If you are anything like me, I have to have something get me to practice what I just read. So I included several in this exercise.

Monday
Help! No Boss

Idea: What is the hardest part about owning your own business?
   No one to…
   ➤ Hand you a paycheck
   ➤ Tell you when to work & when to get off work
   ➤ Tell you to take a break
   ➤ Tell you what to do next or where to go
   ➤ Give you that days action plan
   ➤ Motivate you
   ➤ Pat you on the back
   ➤ Push you out of your comfort zone

Story: In 1999, I went from running my retail store which I knew I needed to arrive by 9AM to get the store ready every morning and left at 10 every night after clean up. I knew pretty much what I needed to do every day of the week to make the store function and produce a profit. I didn't have any requirements, a particular time I needed to get up or leave, who to call, what to do first or any structure at all. Wow, what an adjustment. I created a rough schedule to give myself some idea each day how to continue to move forward in this new adventure.

Points: Mark an appointment book, sheet or online scheduler by half hour increments. Now go and schedule out your entire day. When will the alarm goes off, when to have breakfast, get ready, get kids to or from school, check e-mails, return phone calls, take a break, take a lunch break, exercise, work on your website, work on social media, work on paper work, attend networking activities, schedule meetings with alliance partners or potential new clients, cold call, attend events and conferences, get off work, eat dinner, play with kids or pets, take care of chores, connect with spouse, watch TV, get ready for bed, go to bed, read, etc.

Action Points: Don't leave out anything. Don't forget to schedule in travel time between activities. Soon you won't have to schedule it out to the extreme but it is good practice to do it at least once for a week. You will be surprised how much time you waste, how much is spent on areas that do not produce income and where you can improve your schedule so that you aren't just busy all day but you are working on your success in life, family, health and your business!

Tuesday
<u>Are you letting Fear Control You?</u>

Idea: Who is in charge in your life and in your business? Are you letting fear overwhelm you and keep you from doing something that you know would be great for your development or your business? What is holding you back?

Story: I knew a lady who had a horrible life. She had every right to have every fear imaginable. She had a speech impediment, her parents got divorced and remarried which had its own emotional challenges, she had cancer, was robbed and tied up, her business was violated by a huge break-end, attacked by people she called friends and those weren't even the worst parts. You might be saying... no way someone could recover from all of that.

WELL... I DID!

What I decided was that all of that was my past and it would not ruin my future. I knew tackling my fears would be hard but I knew that, if I wanted to grow and be the person I wanted to create, I would have to transform my thoughts and actions!

Points: Make a list of your fears and get ready to tackle them! Then next to your list, write out beside each fear the positive result that could happen if you pushed through that road block.

Action Points: Find a caring face or someone to lean on if you must. Let them know you are feeling weak about this task. Make sure they will push you to do it anyways. You will be amazed as to what you can do! Take a deep breath and just go for it!

So who is going to be the winner?

You Are The Winner!!!

No Fear is going to keep you from succeeding!!!

Wednesday
Mistakes and Failures

Idea: Over and over I hear how people keep from doing something because they are fearful that it will fail or it is a mistake. How do you know? Until you try something, you really don't know. Also, most of the richest people in the word have tried something that was a miserable failure. The difference is if you learn something from it. We wouldn't be where we are today without the successes and the failures of yesterday.

So how do you satisfy your mind's subconscious to want to stay safe but then take the risk anyways? Make a knowledgeable conclusion. Figure out the real risks and find people who can help you assess those risks. But no matter how much you assess an idea, at some point you have to make a decision. At some point you have to say, I believe in this new idea and I'm going for it or I'm scraping it.

Story: Wow, which failure to pick! I try new ideas out all the time. Once I decided to create a travel series that I was going to air on the Travel Channel. Well, that was the plan at least. I went into a partnership with a former friend. Yes, former... don't go into business with an equal partner. We had it all ironed out and ready to move forward. Then her husband gave her a new idea and the entire business plan changed over night. They said that this was the only way which was completely different from our original plan. I learned a lot from the experience and was sad that it ended our relationship.

Action Point: Is there something you have wanted to try or accomplish? What is holding you back? Find a group of people and ask them their thoughts. Ask everyone and listen. Making a decision quickly can be a good thing or a bad thing but either way, what are the facts and what do you want out of it. But put your personal feelings about the subject on hold and really listen. Don't get offended or offensive with those you ask or it may be the last time you can ask them and always thank them for their feedback.

Point: Don't be so afraid of making a mistake that it keeps you from trying. There will always be people that will put down your ideas. Find a group that will encourage you and give you great feedback. Give your idea a shot. Ask questions, get a game plan and give it a try!

Thursday
Afraid of Rejection

Idea: Yes, the ugliest word in our vocabulary. Rejection! Who wants to be rejected especially over and over again? Of course no one, but it is a reality of being in business. The biggest reason is that we are talking to people that are not our target market. The narrower your target market the less likely you are going to be rejected but that also relies on you. If you are talking to the right market of people, they will be much more open to what you are offering or selling.

Story: I was at an after-hour networking function and everyone who attended received a drink ticket and a huge buffet of all kinds of sugary delights. There was a lady working the crowd and, as I watched her and the reaction of the people she walked up to, I was intrigued as to why everyone went from smiling to frowning within seconds of meeting her. I walked over to her and I could tell she was upset at her response she was getting. I asked her what her business was and she went into how she was a nutritionalist and how bad the wine I was drinking and the yummy items on my plate were for me. I kindly suggested that she change her approach to networking and pick a more suitable group. I explained that people were there to enjoy themselves and not be scolded. She hadn't thought of it that way.

Points: Look at your Target Market breakdown. Where can you go that there is more a likelihood that your target market will be there? If you get a negative vibe, get out of there.

Also, remember that not everyone will like you. Ooohhh, that is a hard one especially for women. Yes, it is true. Not everyone will like you and there will be people who can't stand you and, as you build your business, you will get more and more of them. But that won't keep you from succeeding. For one thing you will be amazed by more people that will admire you and want to be around you!

I always thought it was weird that someone didn't like me... I mean what's there not to like, right? But I came to the realization that it isn't me, it is them. So I stopped sweating about it.

Action Points: How are you going to target your market to be around the people who are more likely to want your product or service? This week, figure out where that place is and try it out. While you are there, ask the people there where else they would suggest you go to find other fabulous people like themselves.

Monday
Comfy Zone

Idea: Who doesn't like to snuggle up and stay where all things are familiar and comfy? Everyone does! But to move forward in your business you have to make yourself uncomfortable as much as possible. You can't make a sale or create connections, if you don't get out and jump into a zone or two that isn't your safe spot.

Story: My husband and I made an agreement with each other that we weren't allowed to get comfortable and to always be learning and challenging ourselves. Now I've got to admit that there are times I'm ready to be comfy and coast, but I know that nothing ever happens when you are on cruise control. It is once you hit the accelerator when something exciting happens. One day I was playing Spider Solitaire (which is my weakness) when I decided to stop and send a hello e-mail to a lady I hadn't reached out to in awhile. She immediately e-mailed back that she had been thinking of me and wanted to reconnect. We instituted a new alliance plan and I received an amazing new client and connections from it.

Points: What is your dreaded comfort zone? Is it the TV or housework? Is it your e-mails, social media, or video games? Is it fears that hold you back? Make a little note on a sticky pad and put it up on your monitor or TV or whatever is our default area and tell yourself "You Can Do It!" You have to fight the urge to run back into your easy chair or sit in a corner at an event and not talk to anyone.

Ask yourself what could you do if you didn't play solitaire today? My favorite quote is "Life isn't about Finding Yourself, Life is about Creating Yourself!" (unknown author) So who do you want to be? Who do you want to create today and what would that do for you, your life, your health, your family, your business, etc.? Imagine the possibilities!

Action Point: So this week, define what is keeping you from jumping out of your comfort zone and creating a winning and successful business professional! What will be your game plan to get off the couch or walk into a room or cold call on that fantastic new client? Who are you going to create from this point forward and write it down! Put it up where you will read it every day. Go for it!

Tuesday
Growth and Change

Idea: Most of us don't like change; which makes growing really hard. We have to surround ourselves with new ideas, new possibilities, new procedures and a new business models as we grow our business. This is what keeps most people at the "I'm struggling in business!" level forever! They won't ask for, want or demand change.

Story: When I owned my retail stores, my father asked us one day what our P&L statement looked like. Of course we said fine even though we had no idea what that meant. We had to learn what was profit, loss, how to assess it and what it all meant for our business growth. We also decided to look at what we were ordering for the store. I was shocked because when my husband asked me to tell him the top ten selling items in the store, not one of them I gave him was actually on the real spreadsheet! We also looked at the top ten most profitable items and again were shocked. We learned the hard way to ask questions and find out things we just had not learned yet.

Points: Get a good solid base of knowledge to work from. Grow into each arena step by step. Don't try to skip steps, it will eventually come back to haunt you. Don't expect to be the top person in your industry that took the top person 20 years to get where they are and expect to be there in a year. Have realistic goals. Is it really that bad to wait ten years for a million dollar paycheck versus always starting over and never getting off Go? There are a lot of steps to business and more importantly personal growth and development.

Action Points: So what is keeping you back from growing? Is there a part of your business that you know will free up time, energy, money and you are avoiding doing something about it or finding someone to help? This week really dive into what is holding you back and you can't just say "Money." Is it sales, marketing, a better website, learning social media or getting uncomfortable? Start to tackle it and grow!

Wednesday
Cold Calling vs. Networking

Idea: I have had people explain that they can't stand cold calling but love networking and others who love or can't stand both. There really isn't too much difference except that …

With networking, a set amount of people come to you in one spot.

With cold calling, you have the opportunity to meet a lot of different people but you have to go out and meet them one at a time.

You also build a business relationship in networking with them so that referrals come from their partnership agreement with you. Both are about meeting new people in the hopes they know someone that may need your product/service or even for themselves.

Do you cold call now? You should. How are you going to find new clients? Yes, you can be proactive and do a lot to draw them your way but at some point you will need to talk to someone you don't know about your product or service. Are you networking? You should. How are you going to build the relationships that will send your referrals and cause leaps and bounds of change for you and your business? Both have their respective place in your business.

Story: I always look at a referral as a bonus. People who say they only have a referral based business to me mean they don't want to market themselves! Yes, who wouldn't want people coming to you from other means so you don't have to prospect but that takes time and connections to build? I try and figure out a great way to talk to a new prospect that is different than anyone else. A gentleman I know who does printing and graphic design wraps chocolate bars with his contact info. When he goes into a new business, he always brings in two bars; one for the boss and one to leave with the nice secretary. It works like a charm.

Points: To grow your business you can't stay in your home or office and hope that the perfect client will walk into the door. Just because you built your company doesn't mean that people will come flocking. Mostly it is about expanding your market and getting people to know who you are. Also, talking with incredible individuals who may be a great source of referrals or even a sale is a huge plus every day.

Action Points: Find a networking group, chamber, industry association near you. Go. Be friendly and don't sell. Ask for a coffee meeting with those who are your competition or have your same target market first and then move on from there.

Second, walk into someone's store and don't sell to them. Just find out about them. I bet that before the conversation ends, they will ask you about what you do. Be willing to connect them to someone who would make a great alliance partner or customer if you know someone. Take the first step and don't get discouraged if it isn't the crowd for you or the person rejects you flat. Move on to a better pond!

Thursday
The Most Important Thing to Do

Idea: So what is the most important thing you can do for your business success? It is simple: Make others feel important! From your potential new clients, your existing clientele, alliance partners, employees and to random people you meet. The reason is very simple. Everyone gravitates to people who make them feel special which in turn leads to sales and opportunities.

Story: I was speaking at an event in Houston. I had heard of one of the main speakers but never had the chance to hear her presentation or meet her. I was excited to find her presentation not only motivational but informative. I approached her after the event and told her that I had heard so many nice things about her and her speaking skills, but also the work she did with business women. That, of course, brought a huge smile to her face and she asked me what I did. We agreed to make an appointment after the event to talk further. We reconnected a week later and after explaining how I wanted to help her connect with other speaking opportunities, she gave me a huge connection! I love helping people feel great about themselves and what they do!

Points: It costs you nothing to be nice to someone and they will remember your kindness much longer than you will remember doing it. When people talk positively about you when you aren't around then you know you are doing a great job of being a positive force in their lives. When someone does something well, give them a compliment and change their day for that moment. Some people go through their entire life never hearing an encouraging word. Wouldn't you love to change that?

Action Point: So, review your approach to people. Do you give a lot of thank you's each day? Do you smile and congratulate people or does that make you feel like it devalues your success if others are succeeding? Do you hear from others that people talk positively about you? Is the chatter always negative? So go out and approach each day by saying, "Who can I affect in a positive way today?" Go out of your way to make someone's day!

Look at this week as the week that is about others. Go out of your way to post something nice about someone on your social media accounts. Say "Thank You" to everyone who deserves it and tell them that you are appreciative of their efforts. You will be surprised how it makes you feel and how positive it changes your attitude. Don't expect a lot of positive action back your way right away, but in time it will come!

Monday
Time Management: Arrive Early

Idea: Look at your schedule for all of your appointments for your business day. Are they back to back? Are you dropping off kids or leaving at the last moment in the morning and then not stopping all day long? Most new business owners feel like they have to max out every minute to be productive. Most people feel that if they squeeze in every minute to meet people that they are going to get the most out of every day. This is simply not true. There is so much that rests on appearances that will dictate if you make the connection or close the sale that day.

Story: It is crazy how many stories I have about arriving early and meeting someone unexpectedly. Stories of someone who took two and a half hours but closed at the end and I had given myself plenty of time between people for the long winded person. My favorite story is a time I went to the local coffee shop and arrived about 45 minutes early. I set up and was ready. A guy next to me saw my business card I had placed on the table for the "person coming." He asked me what I did, had a great conversation, set an appointment with him for later and closed the sale at the appointment with him.

Points: If you are early, you also have the control. They are walking into your world versus you coming in to theirs. The appearance that you have everything under control gives you the upper hand in the whole situation.

It may seem impossible to squeeze in an extra 15 to 30 minutes in between every appointment but give it a try. You will be surprised how you feel at the end of the day with extra time to collect yourself and be ready. There is never any reason to be late. Give that person you are meeting with the respect of making them feel like they are more important than anything else by giving them the gift of your time.

Action Points: Look at your schedule… are you a squeezer or a controller? It is simple; learn to be in control of your day. That is one of the reasons that you are an entrepreneur, right? If most of your meetings are an hour then give yourself two hours for drive time and arriving early and leaving late. Also try and put as many appointments in the same place as possible but don't back-to-back those appointments either. If you are about to make the deal happen and the next person comes in for their slotted time, then guess what… you lose the sale or upset the next person and lose that sale. So give yourself the gift of time, control and less stress!

Tuesday
Time Management: Time to Let Something Happen

Idea: Most people live their life filled to the max and running from one thing to the next. From the moment that the alarm goes off, they have a full agenda and off they go. What if you gave yourself a moment for something magical to happen? Something completely unexpected presented itself to you without any plan at all.

If you are running from one event to the next without time to breathe then you are missing out. You are frying your nerves and missing opportunities that may be all around you. Stop and smell the roses. Stop and enjoy moments because you will never have those moments again. Sounds silly in the business world but it is true that the more you isolate yourself from opportunities the less likely those opportunities will happen.

Story: The craziest part of meeting new people that you just bump into accidentally is the amazing connections they have, opportunities, ideas or even a sale. I was at a local coffee shop again and my meeting had wrapped up and I had about 30 minutes between appointments. I looked around and the guy beside me looked over and smiled. I smiled back and asked him if he worked around there. After he talked for about ten minutes about his new business he was launching, he asked me about mine. The conversation led to how he could get involved and signed up right there. How exciting to make not only a sale but a great new connection out of the blue!

Points: Are you losing out on amazing moments? Do you feel like you have to fill every minute of the day or you aren't being as productive as possible? Reevaluate your schedule and see where there is space to stop or arrive early.

Action Points: Take this week's schedule or start from this point on and give yourself 15 to 30 minutes between meetings or activities and this does not include drive time. Realize that you also must utilize this time too. Use it to talk to people you run into. Find time to meet three new acquaintances a day by giving yourself time to say "Hi!" At the end of the year you will have a lot more connections and possibilities!

Wednesday
<u>Are You a Positive Person?</u>

Idea: Do you look at things in a positive way? Are you sure? Most people talk negatively without even knowing it. Appearance is everything but even more than what you appear to be is what you say you are. If you sound like you are struggling in your business and every little thing is a negative then people will avoid you. Most people only want to be around positive people. They want to walk into a room and see smiles and not frowns. Which do you wear?

Story: This was a hard thing to do for me. People would ask me how I was doing and I would really tell them! Finally I hired a coach that simply told me, no one wants to know how you are actually doing. They are just starting a conversation. I stopped focusing on the reality of my situation and instead on the real positive things that were happening in my life. Boy, did it make a huge difference in people's approach to me and my sales!

Point: How do you see things? When you fill up your gas tank are you cursing the price of gas and having to spend the money again or are you thankful you used all of your gas to meet new people, build your business, create revenue, learn something new, and go some place you haven't been before? Listen to what you say to others. Is it a negative? Most of the time we can't hear ourselves so find someone who can critique your statements.

Action Point: Go through this week and really try to find the positive in everything. This is harder to do than you think! Most of us have been in such a negative environment for so long it is hard to find something good to say about everything. I will tell you that there is always a silver lining. ALWAYS! So go out and find the good in everything and enjoy the positive nature that will give you and your business.

Thursday
Who Do You Surround Yourself With?

Idea: There have been a lot of studies on how the people around someone affect their life and their success. All of the studies show that the people that you surround yourself with are exactly like you in mind set, success and income within a degree or two. Who are you surrounded by?

Story: In the beginning of 2011, I stopped and evaluated my business and personal growth. I had accomplished so much but seemed to be coasting and not growing any more. I realized that the people I was hanging around personally were no longer the bigger fish. I had quickly jumped ahead of so many or was at least equal. I knew that I had to find a new group to hang around. At that point, like in the past, I would search around and go to lots of different groups, ask people who I did want to hang out with where they went for fun and quickly found my new environment. It was hard, it took time but was well worth the effort!

Point: Look around yourself and review the people that you are always around especially in business. Are you playing with people that are more experienced, wealthier and have more success than you or are you the big cheese in the group? You should always be the guppy and never the big fish so that you have room to grow.

Action Point: So this week review your friends, family, partners, coaches, comrades, acquaintances and look to see if you are the guppy or the big fish. If you are the top dog then you need to start looking for a new group of people to be around. What group is a step up? It doesn't have to be a huge leap but just a step up. When hiring anyone to help you grow, are they more successful than you are? When finding a new friend to hang around, are they more successful than you are? Where you hang out, is it a place where you will meet people that you can learn from? Make a change now!

Monday
Make It Easy

Idea: Most people make sales more difficult than they need it to be. If you are looking at a person in a line at the coffee shop, grocery store, etc. that looks like your perfect client then you must say "Hi." Now let's talk about how to make it even easier! Create a way to have that person say "Hi" to you! How you might ask? Wear a name tag! You can order them online or at a local print shop. Buy a few because you will misplace them, lose them and wash them. Get a magnetic back so it won't ruin your clothes too.

Story: I left a networking group and went over for a coffee meeting right after and still had on my name tag. I was standing in line and the person in front of me turned around and glanced at my name tag. Surprise came across their face and they said... "My friend told me that I need to meet you!" We had a great conversation and booked an appointment to meet.

A different occasion, I ran into the grocery store on the way home one day and was walking along the veggie aisle and went to grab a bag to put my squash in and a gentleman was reaching at the same time. He glanced at my name tag and asked me what I did. I explained, gave him a business card and he contacted me the next day to meet.

Points: So what to say on your name tag?

Company logo, name of company (if the logo doesn't say) and your name! You can also have something clever on it such as "Ask Me What I do!," "I Talk to Strangers," "I'm Shy So Say "Hi," "Are you looking for a new home/to look younger/better car insurance...," "Hi, My name is _____!"

Make it easy to read! Don't make it cursive, cluttered, or too much color. You want the person to glance at you and be able to read it in one second! I've seen ones that blink, scroll with whole messages or worn upside down. Don't make it a negative! You don't want to take that the amazing first impression and be looked at as a "what" or a "why." You want them to meet you and say "Hi, ___ your name___. It is nice to meet you." This is productive instead of a long drawn out conversation about your name tag and why you are wearing it upside down or they are waiting forever to read one word at a time (which they won't sit and do).

Make sure you wear your nametag on the right side between your heart and your collar bone. Ladies, don't force people to look at your boobies; guys you too. Make sure it is straight. If it starts to fade or wear out then get a new one. Keep your image professional.

Action Points: So buy a few name tags that are easy to read. Wear it anytime you leave your home. You will be amazed how many people will want to talk to you!

Tuesday
How to Approach People

Idea: I see it all the time. I can tell when someone wants to say "Hi" but they just won't take the steps. Most people are really nice. Most people aren't mean and grumpy. Most people would love to have a great conversation with a stranger that day. So how do you approach someone without making them feel like you are attacking or just weird?

Story: I asked a guy once when he was going to sit down at a table next to me what he did as a coach since I saw his embroidered shirt that mentioned a name of a coaching firm. I ended up not only with an appointment but when his appointment came in for their meeting, at his table he introduced me and I made an appointment with his guest too!

Points: Here is a list of things you must do:
1. Smile
2. Have eye to eye contact
3. Approach directly & confidently

How to start a conversation:
1. If they sneeze say "Bless You" or whatever your response is.
2. Don't I know you?
3. Didn't I meet you at that networking group, chamber, party, conference, etc.?

4. Do you have the time, date, etc.

Once you have their eye contact, you have them smiling back and you have your first conversational response you have now moved it to the permission stage to start a full conversation. Don't fret if the person is unresponsive, never smiles, goes back immediately to what they were doing before. Move on to someone else!

Remember in order to keep the conversation going, the conversation must be about them and not your business! Hopefully you are wearing your name tag and if they want to ask you a question they will. Keep the conversation about them and how you can help them, but help does not mean what your product or service will do for them. Only when they ask you what you do or who you are do you say anything about your business! Believe me, those who don't ask are not your target market and not worth telling anyway!

Action Points: So go out and see who you can help today! Put yourself in the long lines and sit in the middle of the action! You will be amazed that when you are helpful and nice that others will appreciate it and want to find out more! They even may want to do business with you, but remember that first they have to like you and they can't like you if they never meet you!

Wednesday
Meet 3 New People a Day!

Idea: So the concept is basic. The more people you meet the more sales you will have. It is a huge sales funnel! At the top is the amount of people it takes to equal at the bottom one sale. This all depends on your closure rate. Realize that it takes even a really great sales person around three months to get really great at presenting and closing the sale. Do you know your average?

Story: My goal each day is no less than three new people to meet that I haven't met before or even need to reconnect with. Everyone's life changes drastically every six months so talking with past acquaintances is a fantastic idea! To make it easy on myself though, I opt to try and find people while I'm already out. It makes it so much easier than making a special trip to prospect.

I meet people while I'm meeting others for an appointment, while having lunch or dinner, while grocery shopping, clothes shopping, at the kids school waiting for them to come out for pick up, at events I'm attending, getting gas, or wherever I see someone I don't already know! I have met incredible people because I saw an opportunity to say "Hi!"

Points: So let's look at the funnel more closely. Say that you need to talk to 50 people to set ten appointments. And it takes five people to gain one sale. So your average leans to ten percent and as you get better at talking to people that ratio changes. So now it only takes two people to make a sale. That decreases it by 50 percent. But what you didn't think about and what we will be covering later is how to turn the people who are not interested into someone who will refer business to you!

Action Points: So look at this weekend and next week, where are you going to be at to meet a lot of people. Is your target market in your scenario? That will take that 50 people way down for appointments to be set because you are talking to the right people. Remember our chocolate chip cookie example? The better you are at figuring out who wants your cookie the easier it is to make those appointments and sell your product or service!

Thursday
How to make them feel comfy!

Idea: We've touched a little on how to talk to people who you don't know. This even applies to people you do know and how to make them feel so comfortable with you that they want to find out more. The entire key is not to make them feel like you are selling to them. Even informing them is too much. Your most important job is to remove their defenses so that you can have a great conversation about their wants.

Story: I met a lady at a fundraising event. She approached me with a huge smile and I was at first intrigued. Then she opened

147

her mouth and said "I heard you are someone I need to know and since you know so many people you can help connect me to people who need to be really healthy!" She went on to explain in great detail about her new health line and how it could help so many people I knew. Now, she didn't try selling to me but trying to sell to people I know has the same effect of nothing ever happening. She did show enthusiasm but she lacked tack. She never received those contacts because I didn't know her, she didn't take the time to know me and she didn't give a sense that she was going to be a team player or help people I knew except to sell them.

At the same event, I had someone else come up to me with almost the same approach but much more effective. "I was told by Patty that you know a lot of people. I would love to hear how you were able to meet so many and about your business." She never told me what she did until we made an appointment and actually sat down to talk. She did a health line and I was able to connect her to someone I knew who had mentioned that he was looking for a better vitamin line.

Points: So how do you approach people? Do you approach them with your palm facing up or thumb facing up? This is figuratively of course! Is your approach to everyone about you and what you do or is about them and their needs? Are you droning on and on and the person you are talking to rolling their eyes to the ceiling? Are you even really looking at the person and gauging their reaction to what you are saying? Are you giving them the respect they deserve? Most people are so caught up in themselves they forget that sales is never about you but always about the other person!

Action Points: Next time you meet someone new; approach them with respect and kindness. Make it about them and only bring up about your business if they ask. If they do ask, keep it short and to the point. Leave the dissertation at home. Ask the questions about them, their business or anything other than yourself or your business.

Monday
<u>Always let them go first!</u>

Idea: When you present your product or services, have a one-on-one meeting, meet someone for the first time or any opportunity where you will be talking about your business and its products and/or services, let the other person talk first. Even if they sit down and ask you what it is that you do, turn the conversation immediately around and ask them a question to focus the conversation back on them. This is so that you stay in control and you can see what type of person is sitting/standing in front of you and how they like to have a discussion.

Story: I'm sitting and waiting on an appointment. The lady rushes in and when she plops down she immediately says, "I'm so excited to meet you and find out about your business. So what is it all about?" Now, I could have gone into my whole presentation which we all have the tendency to jump right into. I fought back my urge and switched gears by asking her "I'm so glad to meet you too! I heard you are a fantastic realtor. So what part of Austin do you cover?" I was so glad I did, she was a story teller and went into details about what was important to her such as her kids, her background and her business. That way when it was my turn, I knew to talk about my kids, pets, where I was from, how I got here and about my business.

There was another meeting where the gentleman wanted to meet at his office. Again, I walked in and he said, "I'm so glad that we were able to get together so tell me all about your business." I had to fight back the urge since he seemed so eager to hear about my business but I stopped and asked him, "Thanks for inviting me, so do you cover everything for insurance?" He was short and to the point, he talked about ROI (return on investment) and lots of business terminology. Nothing was said about the past, present or personal so I kept my presentation short, sweet and to the point!

Points: Have you given time to listen to how someone is talking to you? Are you matching their style to your presentation? People want to be comfortable with the person in front of them and they want to relate so the better job you do at listening to their style the better! You will be amazed to how easy it is to connect with someone you don't know when you meet them in their comfort zone.

Action Points: So, on your next appointment, next time you meet someone new or give an elevator pitch on what you do and what your business is, make sure the other person goes first! They will also remember your conversation longer if you go last. Remember, a sale is never about you and your needs, but always about the other person's wants and comfort level!

Tuesday
<u>How to Listen</u>

Idea: The ability to listen and react is the basis of all sales. If you don't stop and hear what the needs and desires are of your potential new client then relationship ends up being about you and you sell nothing! Are you having a hard time closing sales? Is it because you are using the words: We, My, Mine, Us, Our! Phrases such as, "We can do this for you." "My products are amazing." "You should join us." "Our new product blows away the competition!" So what does the person really want and why are they listening to you in the first place? Do you know and did you listen to what they said?

Story: When I would sell my online marketing and advertising directory ads, I would have clients go first and then I'd ask them questions throughout their presentation. Once I was having a great conversation with a local business coach. He went first and as he talked about his business, I could see he was excited about telling a lot of people. I asked "Do you speak and do presentations?" He got very excited and told me that he wanted to really get into a lot of speaking engagements. When it was my turn to give my presentation, one of the services I focused on was my Speaker's Circuit. I was able to satisfy a true want in his life and he bought.

Points: People will tell you everything IF you listen and ask. They will lead you exactly to where you need to go but you won't know where that path is unless you listen carefully. Did you ask precise questions to help the path become even clearer? Are you taking notes to remember and know what to focus on in your presentation? Are you talking about something they just said that they weren't interested in?

For example: If you sell a line of cleaning products and the potential new client just said they don't like cleaning because you mentioned that you love making the house tidy then if you focus on your cleaning products you have not only lost her as a client but anyone she would have referred to you. Instead you ask another question, such as "I was so glad when I found a way to save time on laundry... don't you love it when you have time left over at the end of the day?" That could lead into a great conversation. You can even ask what her hobbies are and what she does with her free time.

Action Points: So, the next time you are with someone let them speak 90% and you speak 10%. Listen, take notes and care about what they are telling you. Do you have a question or two that will help you identify what products or services would be best for them? Have questions already figured out that would be great to ask people. In that way you are prepared when the conversation doesn't go a direction that easily leads to a sale.

Wednesday
Turn Conversations into an Appointment

Idea: So the whole point of meeting new people is to set those appointments that may turn into a sale! A conversation should always lead to an appointment. Remember that conversations are not presentations. Never present unless it is an actual sales appointment or one on one meeting, unless of course they ask you to.

Story: I was at an event and a vendor booth I approached asked me for my e-mail address. Since the card had my business name on it, the person behind the table asked me what my business was all about. I gave a short little elevator pitch and told him that I would love to learn more about his business. I asked him right there if he had his appointment book with him and he did. We set an appointment before I walked away.

I was at a networking group and, after my presentation I was giving that day, I stayed behind and met two new ladies that wanted to talk to me about my business. I asked each of them if they had their calendars in front of them and if we could make an appointment so we could really get to know each other and find out more about each others businesses.

Points: Always have your calendar ready. Not only will it show others you are prepared but you can get appointments booked on the off chance you run into someone new! It takes a lot more effort to follow up than to set the appointment up front. Always ask them for the appointment, tell them that you want to find out more about them and how you can help them and then (the most important part) tell them that you would like to tell them a little about your business too.

Make sure you have the understanding up front. Before I would just say I want to find out more about them and their business and then after they told me at the appointment about them and their business they would leave and not want to know about mine. When I changed it and made the agreement that they would also have to listen to what I had to say too, then my sales went through the roof.

Action Points: So the next time you meet someone new, ask them if they would like to get together. Pull out your appointment calendar to figure out the time and what part of town you will be in at the time and day they want. Try to schedule meetings at the same location or close to it so that you don't have to run all over town. If they are down south and you are up north, then figure out a spot in between. Make sure you know most of the coffee shops and lunch locations across town so you can immediately give a suggestion. Make sure you take into consideration the time of day with traffic and school zones. Show up early, get ready to listen and make that sale or great new referral partner!

Thursday
Ask Questions

Idea: Most people know that the best way to present and sell is to ask the prospect questions. The best way is to ask specific questions throughout the presentation and the "get to know you" time to drive the conversation in the direction you want it to go. You must learn to control the questions and then you will have more success in closing. We've talked a little about asking questions during their time to talk about who they are and what they do but let's go to the next level.

Story: I was at an event I sponsored and had a booth there. It was very slow and it was mostly an art show. Most of the people who came in to walk the vendor area were W2 employees and, since I'm looking for people who want to own, start or have their own business, the people coming by my booth weren't really my target market. However, the other vendors were. So I would go to each booth and start a conversation about their products, artwork, and the city we were in. I would stay in control of the conversation the whole time. For example:

> 1. I asked how business was so that I could talk to them about my coaching
> 2. Did they have a lot of traffic and sales on their website so that I could talk about my website programs?
> 3. Do they go to a lot of events like this so that I could talk to them about being a leader and running my booths for free?

I made some key connections and was able to follow up with each one of them on their specific interest.

Points: What questions do you need to ask? Be careful not to ask too personal of a question. Ask general questions that you can drill down later. Are you talking to someone you just met, that you are having a one-to-one, a full presentation or a follow up conversation? This will also depend on what you ask. The more you prepare what you want to ask and where you want to lead them then it will help you be ready in any situation.

Action Points: Write down questions that people like to answer. The questions must be about them and their needs/wants. Feel comfortable asking the questions and see if you can do it very casually. If the questions seemed rehearsed or forced, people will know you are fishing for answers. All of this is for one reason, how can you best help that person today; however, the answer may be, you can't. No worries, there are plenty of other fabulous people out there that you can help.

Monday
Don't Factor

Idea: Some of the best advice I can give you is the "Don't" factor! When selling in person, on your website, over the phone, in an ad, on social media, etc., there are some things that you never ever want to do! Don't preach, teach, put down or talk about your competition! I've got so many stories it could fill a book on this subject so let's explain.

Story: I made a special trip to meet a lady way out in the country. I was interested in her products and she seemed a delight over the phone. When I arrived, she was waiting and was well put together. I was so excited to meet a professional and then she opened her mouth! She started by preaching how I was slowly killing myself with the products I use because I wasn't using hers. She then asked me what I used and began insulting that company and then she went into wanting to teach me all about the benefits of her products. Of course, I walked away and didn't buy a thing.

I met with a gentleman who represented a line of insurance products and financial services; he whipped out a form for me to fill out that covered all of my personal information. I was just meeting him for a one-to-one and felt attacked. I never filled out anything. I didn't know him except for meeting him at a networking event, I sure wasn't going to discuss any of my personal information on my first encounter and his flip chart presentation could have been saved if he just had asked me a few questions first. He realized when I wasn't filling everything out that he had crossed a line but it was one of his first one-to-ones so I filled him in on networking protocols. He ended up later being one of the most connected and amazing networkers out there! Everyone starts from the beginning and we all make mistakes.

Points: So are you always on the attack? Relax for one thing. If you let the other person go first, it will help you know what to cover. Never insult someone! Don't tell them or imply they are stupid, lazy, unhealthy, poor, etc. Never talk about your competition because people are usually very loyal in nature to whatever product or service they are using. So again, don't call them stupid for using that product or service! Just explain what yours does, doesn't do and lead from there. Use examples but never preach. Also, don't go over technical information unless you have realized that your prospect is super analytical and asks you for more information! Lead the conversation by what the person has asked you to cover and what they have stated as being the most important information to them. Also, don't try and be a teacher. People don't appreciate information that they didn't ask for or pay for.

Action Points: So review your approach and how you talk about your products and services. Do you give too much information when all they wanted to know was the price? Did you go into a dissertation when all they wanted to know is what color does it come in or will it help them hurt less? Most people want to keep it super simple. Less is usually always more! If they ask for more, give it to them but if not, keep it short and sweet!

Tuesday
Focus on Positives

Idea: It is important to have your prospects walk away feeling better and not worst. You want to find ways to change people's lives and help them. Focus on what your product or service can do for someone that has a positive outcome. What will excite them to buy your product or service especially if you focus on relieving a pain or discomfort in their life or business?

Story: When I talk to someone about their website needs, I ask them what they are having a hard time achieving in their website. What is their pain? That way I can figure out if there is a way that I can help them. Is it qualified traffic to their website? Then I know to talk about Search Engine Optimization and how they can achieve so much on their own. Is it selling their product or service on line? Then I go into marketing and how things are laid out. Is it uploading images, changing features or content, is it a professional look.

I give examples of what I've seen happen such as a financial advisor who put on his website information trashing a radio show host in his industry. He lost a huge sale because a lady really respected this radio show host and lost respect for the guy who she wanted to work with.

I also want people around me who are positive. I surround everything I do with positive messages rather than on negative messages. This way I can avoid those who thrive in environments of negativity.

Points: So what do you focus on? What images does your website have, your marketing literature, your slogan, etc.? What are they saying about you and your company? Do you seem to be always attracting negative people? Have you looked into why? Is it the words you use? If you can't see it, then ask someone else to tell you what they see. Most of the time we are the worst person to see our own mistakes and our own negativity. Are you focused on your own message, products, services, images, bio, YOURSELF? Most people are. Focus on others and giving them a positive image of you and you will increase sales.

Action Points: So take a look at your website, your marketing fliers, what you post on your social media accounts and really be honest with yourself. If you didn't know yourself and you went to your website or was handed your flier, would you do business with yourself? Are you saying anything that would attract you and then are you like most people out there? How can you tweak things to excite people to give you a call? Figure this out and you have accomplished what the huge marketing companies do everyday.

Wednesday
Focus on Benefits

Idea: We've talked a little about Benefits versus Features. So let's break it down even more. What attracted you to your product or service? What made you go... "I want to sell this!" That is a great place to start but remember that not everyone is like you so ask others in your company or industry why they got into that industry. Current clients are the perfect group to ask too! They all joined for a reason and you have to be open to what they will say.

Story: Do you remember the lady that I told you about who was bashing the very company that I used and never stopped to ask me anything? Well, this is a perfect example of someone who focused on her features and not benefits. She had an organic product and I was interested because I had tried their bath salts before and LOVED them. But, she never found out about my love of her salt bath crystals. Instead, she focused on what was important to her and the features of her product line. What they were made of, the commission structure, the amount of amazing products that they offer. All I wanted to know is what fragrance the bath salts came in.

Another lady I had contacted to find out if she could help me with a need of mine had a different issue. I wanted to know if her company could do what I wanted it to do. She told me that she was bringing in an expert. When he came in, I found out that he had only been with the company for seven months and when I explained in detail what I needed it to do; he insisted that I listen to a lengthy video presentation and that it would explain everything. The video didn't address anything that I had asked him. The worst part is that he didn't seem interested in finding out the answers to my questions and just wanted an easy sale.

Points: Are you focusing on what your products are made of? Are you going over the stats and pie charts? Are you showing a long presentation that focuses on everything instead of just what the person is interested in? Are you explaining how you are going to accomplish what they want rather than on your end result? For example: You probably don't care what the item is called that will fix your AC unit, but what you do care about is if it will make your home cool again. See the difference? Are you focusing on how much horsepower the car has instead of will you be able to pass someone on the freeway with no problem or go up a huge hill with ease?

Action Points: Look at the way you present your product/service. What do you focus on? Is it about how it will make your client feel or how it is made? Are you only showcasing the technology instead of the end result? Dissect what you say about your business. Always focus on the end result and never on what the road looks like to get there!

Final Chapter
So excited!

I am so glad that you spent this time with me. I know that this is just a first step. It takes so much practice and time to achieve changes and success in your business and more importantly in your self! The one thing to keep in mind is to always have fun. That is why you are in a sales position and/or own your own business. I want to meet new people and learn about them, learn from them and challenge myself with their ideas and view points. The hardest part has always been and will always be getting over my fears. It is a challenge. But I'd rather do something daring today where I could possibly change someone's life, attitude, expectations, beliefs, or just turn a frown into a smile than sit by myself waiting for things to happen TO me. I'd rather be a lot more proactive than that. Everyone has the same abilities to affect someone today. Do something nice, say something nice to someone not expecting it, and watch how the day becomes a little bit nicer for you and everyone you talk to.

So join the Positive, Professionals Movement! We can all make a difference. Who says that being in business has to be about clobbering your competition, or you have to be mean and dirty to be in business. Poppycock! We can all work together and change the world.

I hope to meet you soon. Feel free to reach out and say "Hi." Let me know what you thought of the book and something you were able to change or try that made a big difference!

So, who are you going to create today? I'm excited to find out.... Aren't You?!

Tonya

Connect and say "HI!"

Tonya Hofmann
CEO and Founder of
Organization of Power Partners
www.OrganizationOfPowerPartners.com

Social Media Connections:

- facebook.com/tonyahofmann
- twitter.com/tonyaylc
- linkedin.com/in/tonyahofmann

As a bonus for purchasing this book, receive an audio of Tonya Hofmann's 90-minute, live presentation of
"A Client a Day, the Coffee Shop Way!"

Go to…
www.AClientADayTheCoffeeShopWay.com
to receive your link and ENJOY!

CPSIA information can be obtained at www.ICGtesting.com
Printed in the USA
LVOW072231011112

305527LV00002B/3/P